WILD BELIEF

Wild Belief

POETS AND PROPHETS
IN THE WILDERNESS

NICK RIPATRAZONE

BROADLEAF BOOKS
MINNEAPOLIS

WILD BELIEF
Poets and Prophets in the Wilderness

Cover image: sigit wiyono/shutterstock
Cover design: Brad Norr

Print ISBN: 978-1-5064-6463-3
eBook ISBN: 978-1-5064-6464-0

For Olivia, Amelia, and Jennifer

Contents

PREFACE:
What Is the Wilderness?   ix

INTRODUCTION:
Prophecy Revealed in the Wilderness   1

1 TEMPTED:
God in the Desert   15

2 WILD CREATIVITY:
Gerard Manley Hopkins   27

3 STEWARDS OF THE GLORIOUSLY INDIFFERENT:
Wendell Berry and Terry Tempest Williams   47

4 GHOSTS DEMAND MORE:
Jim Harrison and Thomas McGuane   63

5 A TREMENDOUS SUBLIME:
William Everson   83

6 SALVIFIC WILDERNESS:
Mary Oliver and W. S. Merwin   101

CONCLUSION:
A Clearing in the Wilderness   117

ACKNOWLEDGMENTS   131

NOTES   133

INDEX   145

Preface

What Is the Wilderness?

A forest spans behind our house. Bears emerge from the tree line confused. They pace along the high grass and then settle back into the brush. Deer drift across the lawn. They stare down our miniature dachshund, who barks at them from the deck. His mouth dry, he laps water from his bowl and then seems to accept their ghostly presence.

In the distance, vultures make rings around carrion. The occasional red-tailed hawk pauses on a knotted branch. Closer, purple martins swoop around me while I mow the lawn. They dive for bugs loosened by the tractor. Wild turkeys, puffed as if they are proud, gobble while they cross the grass. Our trail camera captures stealthy rabbits, bobcats, and coyotes, who each follow the same paw-worn path into the forest. Foxes, nimble and silent during the day, make what sound like screams in the night.

Snow quiets everything. After a good snowfall, I head into the woods with my wife and daughters. We follow a hunter's path that ends at his tree stand. After that, we move toward the brook, given new life by the snow. Ice curls over both sides, and the girls pitch snowballs into the flow.

The brook turns along a slouched chicken wire fence, leading to a horse farm at one edge of the woods. We watch the horses walk around the paddock while the snow continues to fall, but the canopy of the woods slows the flakes. They sprinkle down rather than churn.

I am drawn to the woods. I spend my working days in a classroom without windows to the outside world, so to return home is a gift. Sussex County, New Jersey, is tucked in the northwest corner of the state, with Pennsylvania on one side, New York on the other. This is not the New Jersey most people know. Much of the county is protected land: forested mountains, deep lakes, and patches of ponds. Streams, kills, and rivers—as bountiful as they are bending. Wild, this land is worth saving.

In 1960, the novelist Wallace Stegner wrote a letter to the Outdoor Recreation Resources Review Commission in support of the Wilderness Act, which would pass several years later—saving and protecting over one hundred million acres of wilderness areas across America. Most conservation efforts appealed to the American sense of play: recreation, leisure, and sport. Stegner had a different idea.

"Being an intangible and spiritual resource," Stegner wrote, the wilderness "will seem mystical to the practical minded—but then anything that cannot be moved by a bulldozer is likely to seem mystical to them."[1] Although swaths of the American wild had already been destroyed, Stegner thought, "Better a wounded wilderness than none at all."[2] Take Robbers Roost in Wayne County, Utah, "scarred somewhat by prospectors but otherwise open, beautiful, waiting."[3] That land "is a lovely and terrible wilderness, such a wilderness as Christ and the prophets went out into; harshly and beautifully colored, broken and worn until its bones are exposed, its great sky without a smudge of taint from Technocracy, and in hidden corners and pockets under its cliffs the sudden poetry of springs."[4]

What, exactly, is the wilderness? Stegner finds enlivening songs in the wild. Others have painted a darker picture. Wilderness, according to Paul Brooks, "remains literally one of the most ambivalent words in the language: it has two contradictory meanings representing two diametrically opposed values."[5] The wilderness is arid, and it is lush. It is forest and desert.

There is no permanent definition for the wilderness; each conception is bound to culture and history. Yet a wilderness must have borders—some porous, some firm. "The idea of 'being lost in the wilderness,'" writes philosopher Max Oelschlaeger, "logically necessitates a geographical referent conceptualized as home as distinct from other places; but for Paleolithic people home was where they were and where they had always been."[6]

Our modern idea of wilderness rests on difference. If we become "lost," we are elsewhere—yet the phrase does not imply someone disoriented deep in the thick woods. We more commonly employ "lost" to mean something, ironically, that we seek. We lose the trappings of civilization so that we might comfortably get lost among nature. Think less threatening expanses and more car camping.

In the Paleolithic world, among "hunters and gatherers," Roderick Nash writes, wilderness could not exist as a concept—for "everything natural was simply habitat, and people understood themselves to be part of a seamless living community."[7] All was wild. But the burgeoning borders of civilization and progress required contrast. The wilderness, then, "became the unknown, the disordered, the dangerous" so that much of "the energy of early civilization was directed at conquering wildness in nature and eliminating it in human nature."[8]

Now we no longer think of wilderness as surrounding us, moving with us. When John Muir wrote in *Our National Parks* that "going to the mountains is going home; that wildness is a necessity; and that mountain parks and reservations are useful not only as fountains of timber and irrigating rivers, but as fountains of life," he assumes a distance between us and the wilderness.[9] The "spiritual values of wilderness"—its mysticism, rejuvenation, transformation—"gain strength as man becomes more urbanized."[10] The more modern we become, the wilder the wilderness feels.

The Bible teems with wild places where faith is tested and reborn. In the Old Testament, the wilderness is portrayed as a place of "covenant, miraculous provision, and judgment."[11] It is a setting, metaphor, story. The biblical wilderness is "not only geographical but psychological"; even the language used to designate wilderness is fluid, implying the wilderness is contextual and preternatural.[12] The biblical wilderness is "primarily used as an absolute noun needing no specifying attribute; it is not a certain locality on the map of the Middle East, but the place of God's mighty acts, significant for all believers of all times and places."[13] If we define it by negation, the wilderness is the opposite of sown places, such as "green pastures, orchards, vineyards, fields, oases, and gardens surrounding the villages and towns."[14] In Isaiah, the wilderness is transformed: "See, I am doing something new! / Now it springs forth, do you not perceive it? / In the wilderness I make a way, in the wasteland, rivers. / Wild beasts honor me, jackals and ostriches, / For I put water in the wilderness and rivers in the wasteland for my chosen people to drink."[15] Jacob was found in the wilderness, that "wasteland of howling desert."[16] Elsewhere, God speaks to Ezekiel: "I will make a covenant of peace with them and rid the country of wild beasts so they will dwell securely in the wilderness and sleep in the forests."[17]

In Matthew, the wilderness is downright devilish: "When an unclean spirit goes out of a person it roams through arid regions searching for rest but finds none."[18] The wilderness poses danger to Paul.[19] When Paul catalogs his sufferings—whipped, beaten, stoned, shipwrecked, robbed, starved—he includes "danger in the wilderness." Although the desert wilderness could be a place of suffering, it was also a place of renewal. From there, the voice of John the Baptist called out, and there, Jesus would retreat to pray—and would also be tempted.

The biblical wilderness, then, is full of "competing ideas."[20] That complex tradition continues in literature and spiritual writing. Dante Alighieri's *Inferno* begins with imagery of the wilderness marked by darkness, fear, and the unknown: "Midway upon the journey of our life / I found myself within a forest dark, / For the straightforward pathway had been lost. // Ah me! how hard a thing it is to say / What was this forest savage, rough, and stern, / Which in the very thought renews the fear."[21] Dante's metaphorical "forest dark" is a necessary route toward spiritual deliverance. He must survive the wilderness in order to reach paradise.

Historically, those who have sought to expand territory see wilderness as "an adversary," and only once "it had been largely subdued could the surviving fragments be enjoyed."[22] As Nash notes, the need to subvert the wilderness came from the union of the biblical vision of that place and the inherent distrust of border spaces. In early and medieval Christianity, "wilderness represented the Christian conception of the situation man faced on earth. It was a compound of his natural inclination to sin, the temptation of the material world, and the forces of evil themselves."[23]

The paradox of the wilderness, though, is that it sustains both visions: foreboding and revelatory. In his preface to *Lyrical Ballads*, written and published as the eighteenth century turned into the nineteenth, William Wordsworth offered critical context for his verse. The "principal object" of his poems was to "choose incidents and situations from common life" in language appropriate to those situations but, "at the same time, to throw over them a certain coloring of imagination, whereby ordinary things should be presented to the mind in an unusual way."[24] He chose "low and rustic life" because those "rural" speakers and characters were direct, concrete, and unpretentious, for "in that condition the passions of men are incorporated with the beautiful and permanent forms of nature."[25] Here Wordsworth's usage of "nature" is interesting; he seems to mean not only human nature but, contextually, also a disposition toward country life. He rejects the poetic artifice of preceding generations that would write of these characters in learned, inauthentic language.

Wordsworth is still a poet, a writer crafting common language into uncommon song. He acknowledges this paradox in his preface and offers a curious way to understand the phenomenon of wilderness and creation. Here the poet must assume a dual, perhaps contradictory, role: he must humble himself to allow common language and experience to become the material of his poetry, yet he must also imbue the magic of imagination and narrative to give structure to that experience. These are not necessarily contradicting impulses or actions. Raymond Williams, who has pondered the evolving idea of nature in culture and language, thought our paradoxical visions of nature were a revelation and not a hindrance: "What in the history of thought may be seen as a confusion or an overlapping is often the precise moment of the dramatic impulse. . . . All at once nature is innocent, is unprovided, is sure, is unsure, is fruitful, is destructive, is a pure force and is tainted and cursed."[26]

Wordsworth's central poetic theory of his preface—that the poet's careful imbuing of imagination transforms the common experience by revealing it—offers a critical framework to understand the wilderness, creation, and faith. John Gatta, in considering the American tradition of writers making nature sacred, offers that it is best to imagine nature "as something both authentically discovered, or discoverable, *and* humanly constructed."[27] Perhaps William Cronon's provocative claim that the wilderness is a "cultural invention" that "offers us the illusion that we can escape the cares and troubles of the world in which our past has ensnared us" is, like the wilderness, both real and unreal, accurate and false.[28] Poets and prophets, united by imagination, capture the transcendent sublimity of the wilderness. Unconcerned with intellectual theories, they capture emotion.

Wordsworth's emotional and narrative sense of wilderness did not always correspond to our idea of vast, untouched expanses. In poems like "The Solitary Reaper," nature and the wilderness are one—united by a woman, "single in the field," who is "reaping and singing" a "melancholy strain."[29] Her entrancing song overflows the fields with sound, and yet her lyrics are unknown. "Will no one tell me what she sings?"[30] the narrator laments. She might sing of "old, unhappy, far-off things" or perhaps some common, "natural sorrow, loss, or pain."[31] Here Wordsworth, the poet who hoped to translate the common song through the transformative power of poetry, offers a narrator who is unable to understand a song of nature. Despite his lack of intellectual understanding, "the music in my heart I bore, / Long after it was heard no more."[32]

The wilderness might be perceived and mapped by us, but it also transcends us. Cronon's criticisms of the wilderness primarily arise from semantic concerns that become ideological—we label impure things wild—but the danger in following those considerations is to neuter the power of the wild.[33]

In America, long before naturalists like Muir would preach the beauty of the wilderness, Native peoples tended "to include the seen and unseen and build upon rather than segregate the sacred."[34] As Joy Porter describes, "Indian approaches to land or place tend to see it as space invested with meaning through lived experience and as something defined by its construction rather than its borders."[35] Muir's effusive, sacral wilderness sense—in an ecstatic 1870 letter, he wrote, "I'm in the woods, woods woods, & they are in *me-ee-ee*"—still hinged on the wilderness as a place that must be reached rather than a home.[36]

"The Indian is indigenous and therefore does not have the psychological burden of establishing his or her right to the land in the deep emotional sense of knowing that he or she belongs there," Vine Deloria Jr. writes—a vision that complicates even complex Western visions of wilderness.[37] Tradition revealed to Native peoples "the sacred landscapes for which they were responsible and gradually the structure of ceremonial reality became clear."[38] Their faith in the wilderness was particular, specific, and born out of the wilderness itself—not projected upon it.

In a different but not contradictory way, for the Transcendentalists, the wilderness was a fount of raw, honest, pure creativity and passion. "In the presence of nature," Ralph Waldo Emerson wrote, "a wild delight runs through the man, in spite of real sorrows."[39] Emerson thought of how "crossing a bare common, in snow puddles, at twilight, under a clouded sky, without having in my thoughts any occurrence of special good fortune, I have enjoyed a perfect exhilaration. I am glad to the brink of fear."[40]

The wilderness can be a place of rejuvenation and wonder—a place where Trappist monk Thomas Merton said, "Man purges himself of 'sediments of society' and becomes a new creature."[41] The human need for wilderness requires conservation and stewardship. The environmentalist Father Thomas Berry once lamented, "We can no longer hear the voice of the rivers, the mountains, or the sea.

The trees and meadows are no longer intimate modes of spirit presence. The world about us has become an 'it' rather than a 'thou.'"[42]

For Berry, the only way to save the wilderness and the wonder therein is to return to our spiritual past: to embrace the "natural world as the primary manifestation of the divine to human intelligence."[43] The "truly sincere, dedicated, and intelligent efforts" of secular conservationists "to remedy our environmental devastation simply by activating renewable sources of energy and by reducing the deleterious impact of the industrial world" are ultimately futile, since they envision the natural world as "primarily for human use, not as a mode of sacred presence primarily to be communed with in wonder and beauty and intimacy."[44] A religious and spiritual vision of the wilderness affirms its immediacy—wind rushing between trees, vines reaching for expansion—and its abstractions. Conservation without these visions loses a broader, eternal scope.

We need the wilderness, and unfortunately, the wilderness now needs us. The poet Gary Snyder thinks such synthesis is inevitable. "Wilderness may temporarily dwindle," Snyder admits, "but wildness won't go away."[45] Snyder paraphrases Claude Lévi-Strauss, saying that "art survives within modern civilization rather like little islands of wilderness saved to show us where we came from."[46] It might be that the more we push and prod and purge the wilderness, the more we long for the wild within us: some natural, raw, sacral faith.

"We need the tonic of wildness," Henry David Thoreau cautioned, "to wade sometimes in marshes where the bittern and the meadow-hen lurk, and hear the booming of the snipe; to smell the whispering sedge where only some wilder and more solitary fowl builds her nest, and the mink crawls with its belly close to the ground."[47] Thoreau's vision was not of a packaged and safe nature; it was of a wilderness in all its surprises and violence. "We need to witness our own limits transgressed," he wrote, "and some life pasturing freely where we never wander. We are cheered when we observe the vulture feeding on the carrion which disgusts and disheartens us, and deriving health and strength from the repast."[48] The wilderness precedes us and will remain long after we die.

The sentiment was evoked well by Susan Fenimore Cooper in *Rural Hours*, her expansive journal of her walks in the New York woods. "Just at the point where the village street becomes a road and turns to climb the hill-side, there stands a group of pines, a remnant of the old forest," she writes.[49] Although changes abound, the pines "stand, silent spectators."[50] Her reflection is tinged with melancholy; she laments how only sixty years earlier "those trees belonged to a wilderness: the bear, the wolf, and the panther brushed their trunks, the ungainly moose and the agile deer browsed at their feet."[51] The personified forest is still, transcendent: a reminder of what is beyond and before civilization.

Wild Belief: Poets and Prophets in the Wilderness looks at poets and prophets, saints and storytellers, who have shown that the natural wild of forests, wetlands, and the desert can bring spiritual transcendence—and that perhaps the tension between our understanding of the wilderness as both a fearful and sacred space makes it particularly apt for capturing the unknown and surprising elements of religious belief. For some of us, the wild world might be distant, but no matter where we live, we feel its natural, ancient, innate rhythms. "The natural world demands a response that rises from the wild unconscious depths of the human soul," Berry wrote; a wildness that is truly God-gifted.[52]

I quote Berry at an especially precarious and strange moment. COVID-19 has spread throughout New Jersey—the state is second only to bordering New York in number of cases. Schools are closed; businesses are shuttered. The woods were an early balm during the crisis. Our local trailhead was packed with cars, trucks, and trailers. Mountain bikers careened past walkers and runners, while those on horseback drifted off trail in silent exploration. These outdoor congregations caught the attention of state authorities, who closed the state parks and trails. Traffic cones line the entrance, and signs warn hikers and runners to keep out.

I miss those wild trails. In the mid-1960s, the Lackawanna Railroad that cut through the county was closed, and the tracks were removed. The routes haunt the woods. Turned into rail trails, the cinder paths are patched with mud and shale, and they cross farmland, border rivers, and swerve around leaning trees. In some sections, wood fires waft from cabins, and horse manure piles like cakes. Cow-trod paths sometimes run perpendicular, while elsewhere, the trails span for miles without other souls. In those sections, rust-caked pickup trucks, gaunt, rest on split tires. Ditched farm equipment is swallowed by the earth.

Before the quarantine, I would run for long miles down those routes, passing old battery boxes and cattail marshes and negotiating footfalls across uneven bridges. When the trail would flatten, long and rootless, I could lengthen my stride. At those moments, exhaustion bleeds into exhilaration, and my mind drifts. I've run on roads and tracks, on grass, and across swaths of farms. I never get the same ecstatic feeling as being in the woods, surrounded by trees. Thoreau was right: we need the tonic of wildness.

Introduction

Prophecy Revealed in the Wilderness

The biblical wilderness is a place of prophecy and revelation, and its climactic story unfolded in first-century Judea. The encounter of two men—John the Baptist and Jesus—was both inevitable and shocking. Their lives and works had been foretold, and yet their identities were confused and blurred. Their interaction would fulfill the heralding of the Messiah and his arrival while establishing a lineage of wilderness narratives of faith that would continue for nearly two thousand years.

"The whole of biblical history," notes George H. Williams, "has, in fact, been interpreted in terms of the wilderness motif."[1] The wilderness illuminates the tension between religion practiced in civilization and a more ancient, wild belief. Wandering sinners yearn for a "second Eden" in that wilderness.[2] The desert, in the Pentateuch, "is the place of God's initial and fundamental revelation to his people."[3] God and Israel are united by covenant in the wilderness. In

Exodus and Numbers, the desert is the scene of "danger and divine help": a location "that threatens the very existence of Yahweh's chosen people, but it is also the stage which brightly illumines God's power and readiness to dispel the threat."[4]

This paradox of suffering and sustenance makes the wilderness a source of endless story. In Numbers 14:33, God says, "Your children will wander for forty years, suffering for your infidelity, till the last of you lies dead in the wilderness." Deuteronomy 8:2–3 is a reminder that "for these forty years the Lord, your God, has directed all your journeying in the wilderness, so as to test you by affliction, to know what was in your heart: to keep his commandments, or not." Wracked with hunger, the people were fed "with manna, a food unknown to you and your ancestors, so you might know that it is not by bread alone that people live, but by all that comes forth from the mouth of the Lord." The people of Israel, through the wilderness, are "not permitted to live in security lest she forget that she is utterly dependent on her God."[5] God's mercy of food does not make a paradise of the wilderness; "the desert situation cannot be forgotten, not even for one day."[6]

Recounted in Psalm 78, the desert strife highlights the stubbornness of man in the face of God. In Psalm 78:19–20, the people spoke against God, saying, "Can God spread a table in the wilderness? / True, when he struck the rock, / water gushed forth, / the wadies flooded. / But can he also give bread, / or provide meat to his people?" The cycle is summarized in Psalm 78:40: "How often they rebelled against God in the wilderness, / grieved him in the wasteland." In these psalmic recountings, "the desert assumes a decidedly darker tint."[7] The desert is both a literal place and a concept: a place "which stands in close proximity to the powers of darkness and death."[8] Williams sees this revealed in Egyptian burial practices where "the dead were not buried in the valuable cultivable land outside the villages and towns, but rather in remote and unwatered places" so that Sheol, "the collective term for all the graves," was "linked with primordial disorder and the withered wilderness."[9]

In the historical books of the Old Testament, "Israel's fundamental belief in her election as God's chosen people" is primarily "rooted in the wilderness tradition."[10] There, David hid as "Saul took three thousand of the best men from all Israel and went in search of David and his men in the direction of the wild goat crags."[11] When Mattathias rejected the decree of Antiochus Epiphanes to make sacrifices to the gods, he "cried out in the city, 'Let everyone who is zealous for the law and who stands by the covenant follow me!'"[12] He fled to the wilderness with his sons and was joined by "many who sought righteousness and justice."[13] It was the wilderness where Elijah journeyed, sat beneath a broom tree, and prayed for death: "Enough, Lord! Take my life, for I am no better than my ancestors."[14] An angel awakens him, and then, after eating and drinking, "he walked forty days and forty nights to the mountain of God, Horeb."[15]

The wilderness of the prophet Isaiah arrives through lyric song. The "redeemed shall walk" through the transformed wilderness, newly teeming with water and flora and free of beasts.[16] The prophet proclaims that God will make the wilderness "like Eden, / her wasteland like the garden of the Lord; / Joy and gladness shall be found in her, / thanksgiving and the sound of song."[17] The Messiah will come from that wilderness: the climactic turn in a long and fractured tale.

The Old Testament themes of the wilderness as a place of journey, struggle, revelation, and transformation are revealed in the Gospels, and there, the Jordan Valley becomes center stage. The valley was rife with narrative, appearing in tradition as "a place of judgement," the "border of the promised land," a "place of divine providence and purification," and a setting for "eschatological restoration."[18] Geographically, the area includes the *ghor*, a "deep, straight, narrow depression" of land, and the *zor*, a heavily vegetated wetland "through which the Jordan river meanders."[19]

There, John became the Baptist. His story begins outside the wilderness, in the village of Ain Karim, where—according to the second-century text *The Protevangelium of James*—John's mother, Elizabeth, had fled in fear of Herod.[20] After the angel Gabriel appears to Mary, she "traveled to the hill country in haste" to visit Elizabeth.[21] Upon Mary's arrival, the infant John leaps within Elizabeth's womb. Filled with the Holy Spirit, Elizabeth proclaims, "Most blessed are you among women, and blessed is the fruit of your womb."[22] Mary stays with Elizabeth for three months, a gentle continuation of the journey theme in which Mary also prefigures her own son's itinerant ministry.

After John's birth, the canticle of his father, Zechariah, affirms that his child "will be called prophet of the Most High" and "will go before the Lord to prepare his ways."[23] John "grew and became strong in spirit" through living in the wilderness.[24] This wilderness could be described as "desolate, empty, lonely land," possibly "stony or sandy, or it may be a grassland."[25] Whatever its exact terrain, John's wilderness was uncultivated land and might have been manned by nomads.[26] This "ascetic preparation" in the wilderness kept John "away from sophisticated religion and politics."[27]

His arrival in public—which begins Mark's Gospel—is framed by this wilderness identity. He "was clothed in camel's hair, with a leather belt around his waist. He fed on locusts and wild honey."[28] His appearance and diet are commonly referenced in passing, but some scholars affirm that his diet reveals much about John's identity in the wilderness. James A. Kelhoffer notes that there is a fine linguistic difference between the accounts of John's wilderness diet in the Markan and Matthean Gospels. In Mark, it is implied that John had the habit of eating locusts and wild honey, while Matthew "makes the more far-reaching claim that John ate only such things."[29] Later in Matthew, the evangelist claims that "Jesus ate and drank like other Judeans, but John did not eat or drink *anything*"[30] and that observers thought John's abstinence was because "he is possessed by a demon."[31] There is a distinction between what John ate in the wilderness (locusts and wild honey) and what he ate in civilization (nothing); this affirms his status in the story as one of the wilderness. Even there, John could have traveled to a location such as Jericho "for supplies"; therefore, "this diet was John's deliberate choice"[32] and "simply a reflection of what was plentiful in his midst: insects and uncultivated 'honey.'"[33] John could have easily gathered locusts on the Jordan riverbank, thus making the wilderness both the source of his personal sustenance and his salvific gift of baptism.

The choice to include food as one of the three introductory characteristics of John—along with his baptisms and his announcement of the one who will bring the Holy Spirit—implies that the Gospel audience "would associate *some* meaning with this cuisine, a meaning that John and his followers may not have readily comprehended, let alone affirmed."[34] The evangelist's audience would recognize the cuisine as "appropriate to the desert, but also a specially holy one devoid of flesh from which blood has had to be drained (hence locusts) and devoid of wine (hence honey)."[35] Steeped in tradition, the audience would similarly have understood his clothing, especially his leather belt, as elevating the "eschatological significance of John's coming as the new Elijah."[36]

Here was a "Jewish prophet who started his ministry before and apart from Jesus, who won great popularity and reverence apart from Jesus, who also won the reverence and submission of Jesus to his baptism of repentance for the forgiveness of sins"—and whose identity was inextricably connected to not only the physical wilderness but also the metaphor and prophecy of the wilderness.[37] His wilderness origin also explains John's mode of speaking. When John proclaims, "One mightier than I is coming after me,"[38] he might be acknowledging that "he existed, both geographically and spiritually, only on the fringes of Judaism, only as a very 'marginal' figure."[39]

John is also "the darker figure" in contrast to Jesus: mysterious in both backstory and method, the prototypical prophet born of the wilderness.[40] His cult in tradition is varied and formidable, with an early admirer being the first-century Jewish historian Josephus, "a student of a Judean wilderness dweller named Bannus."[41] As Josephus wrote, Bannus "lived in the wilderness, wearing clothing from trees, obtaining his food from uncultivated plants, frequently washing day and night with cold water for purity's sake."[42] In fact, some conjecture that "it is not inconceivable that John and Bannus could have known each other."[43]

Josephus's passage about John in *Jewish Antiquities* is "more than twice as long as the passage about Jesus, [and] is also more laudatory."[44] He describes John as surrounded by Jews whose "excitement reached fever pitch as they listened to [his] words."[45] John's rhetorical power caused Herod to fear "some sort of revolt," as Josephus explains that John's crowds "seemed likely to do whatever he counseled."[46]

Herod thought the greatest threat to his rule was a preacher from the wilderness. So powerful was this fear that it continued past John's death. John's criticism of Herod's marriage to Herodias led to the Baptist's arrest. According to Josephus, John was "sent in chains to Machaerus," a mountain fortress in the desert.[47] At first, "Herod feared John, knowing him to be a righteous and holy man, and kept him in custody."[48] Although confused by John's prophetic speech, Herod begrudgingly "liked to listen to him."[49] Herodias's daughter infamously asks for John the Baptist's head on a platter, and Herod, although "deeply distressed," orders the execution.[50]

Yet when word of Jesus's miracles began to spread, they are first attributed to John the Baptist. He is not merely performing miracles; he has been raised from the dead to do so. Mark 6:15 cites others in the conversation who reference the wilderness prophet Elijah. Herod agrees with the rumors: "It is John whom I beheaded. He has been raised up."[51] Herod's attribution of the miracles to John affirms the Baptist's legendary standing. He has come from the wilderness and was charged with abilities not shared by others. He baptized and cleansed in the wild, not in the city. He was killed for his beliefs and the power he had to rally others.

His life and legend had a significant effect on Christian conceptions of the wilderness. Patristic writing is rife with references to John's physical appearance, ministry, and death. Origen wrote that John "was nourished in a new way, not according to customs," and that he was "born in a new fashion and reared in a new fashion."[52] Origen was not quite correct that John's diet was rare, but his misinterpretation has a theological resonance, affirming that John was both foretold and radical. The world was not ready for him.

Origen also thought that John blazed the path for Jesus to the underworld. The Harrowing of Hell, the legend of Christ's descent to the wilderness of hell, was made possible by preparation from John—a theological attempt by the "ancient church to clarify John's place in salvation history by providing a role for him in the extension of salvation to those who died before the completion of redemption."[53] Cyril of Jerusalem also affirmed John's descent. As for John's earthly life, Cyril stressed that John's "garment of camel's hair" demonstrated his "ascetic life" in the wilderness.[54] Sulpicius Severus, the fourth-century Christian historian, wrote of John's influence on the monastery founded by Saint Martin of Tours. Monks, following John's wilderness tradition, "were clothed in garments of camels' hair. Any dress approaching to softness was there deemed criminal."[55] Jerome, a contemporary of Augustine, wrote that Jesus's "forerunner and herald, John, fed on locusts and wild honey, not on flesh—both the habitation of the desert and the initial residence of monks began with such foods."[56] John was not known for his treatises or parables. His teachings were visceral, and his story would become the prototype for the wilderness monk in life, literature, and art.

John's wilderness life offered both literal and metaphorical precedents for believers. While Anthony and other monks hunkered in the Egyptian desert, across the Mediterranean Sea, an Armenian bishop named Blaise lived in the forest of Cappadocia. Blaise had been a physician before he became a bishop, but the persecution of Christians under the reign of Emperor Licinius sent him into the wilderness. According to legend, he found shelter in a cave where injured wild animals flocked to him. Hunters following the blood trail of their prey found the hermit Blaise. On the way to bringing Blaise to the authorities, the group was stopped by a wayward woman who pleaded for help. A wolf had snatched her pig, but Blaise was able to recover the animal unharmed. Blaise was jailed by the governor, but the woman began a devotion to him, bringing him food and also candles to light the dark cell. While imprisoned, he was able to heal a boy who was choking from a fish bone. He was ultimately tortured and put to death, but his memory proved curiously influential and centered on two of his traits: his power over animals and his ability to heal throats.[57]

Starting in the sixteenth century in Germany and traveling elsewhere, Blaise became revered. On February 3, his feast day, throats were blessed with candles tied with red cloth and arranged in the shape of a cross—the opening rested beneath the congregant's throat. In accordance with the saint's healing of the child in the prison, the priest said, "Through the intercession of St. Blaise may God deliver you from ills of the throat and other ills."[58] The tradition continues to the present: a wilderness saint, steeped in lore and healing, whose eremitic life was cut short but whose lineage reflects the appeal of his gifts, the abilities to control wild things and to heal.

The sixteenth-century German painter Albrecht Altdorfer portrayed John in two paintings; in both, he is depicted as a healer coming from the wilderness with mullein, an herb associated with medicinal qualities. Although Blaise has since inherited this devotion, for some medieval Christians, it was John to whom they "prayed for relief from laryngitis and sore throats, and he served as a patron saint for all who invoked his protection from danger."[59] Mulleins were gathered on John's midsummer feast day "and were passed through bonfires in order to drive off evil spirits."[60] The devotion arose from a scant reference in the fourth Gospel, where John is described as "a burning and shining lamp."[61] In Altdorfer's *The Two Saints John*, he depicts the Baptist with a mullein, "known and valued for its usefulness both as a burning torch and as a source of protection and healing."[62] John was an emblem of nature: a bringer of disruption and light. It is no wonder that saints like Blaise produced devotion on similar lines.

While Blaise was becoming one of the most venerated of the Fourteen Holy Helpers—healing saints who were the subject of countless prayers during the plague—a parallel tradition, or perhaps fear, was arising in the medieval wilderness. The wild man was "astoundingly persistent" in medieval art and life. His image adorned "stove tiles, candlesticks, and drinking cups, and . . . house signs, chimneys, and the projecting beams of frame houses," as well as "religious buildings and liturgical books, being found on the borders of illuminated manuscripts, on capitals, choir stalls, baptismal fonts, tomb plates, and as a gargoyle on the eaves of churches."[63]

The wild man was not born of the wilderness; he arrived there. His bestial state "was thus reached not by a gradual ascent from the brute, but by a descent," suggesting the mores of civilization were temporary.[64] Richard Bernheimer reaches back to the book of Daniel for the "insanity of Nebuchadnezzar," who was "driven from men and did eat grass as oxen, and his body was wet with the dew of heaven, till his hairs were grown like eagles' feathers, and his nails like birds' claws."[65] In medieval times, the wild man's madness evolved. He "was now also a prophet, whom his mental waywardness had endowed with oracular faculties, while it compelled him also to forsake human company and to seek shelter in the woods."[66]

A Slavonic translation of Josephus, thought by scholars to include medieval additions, reflects John the Baptist's evolution in legend. He is introduced as one who "wandered among the Jews clad in unusual garments, because he put on furs about his body, on all parts of it which were not covered by his hair."[67] John "looked just like a wild man."[68] His "character was unusual and his method of life was not mortal."[69] After preaching to Jews and baptizing them in the Jordan, John leaves the wilderness to confront Herod in the city. "Pure am I," John says in this account, "for God's spirit has entered into me, and I nourish my body on reeds and roots and wood-shavings"—his wilderness life is used to affirm his holiness.[70] That same wilderness is used by one onlooker to voice skepticism: "You, who have just come out of the woods like a wild beast, how do you dare, indeed, to teach us and seduce the people with your profligate sermons!"[71]

The wild man, an unpredictable prophet who is both human and something else, called to mind any number of perversions.

His wildness was "a temptation, to which one exposed oneself by plunging into the great wild unknown."[72] Although the wild man haunted the wilderness, there is a consistent tradition of those deemed the holiest—saints—making journeys to the wilderness for cleansing and rebirth. The wilderness sustains both traditions: it is a place that men fear and a place that invites transformation. It is, perhaps, the last place on earth where God is viscerally disruptive.

The paradox of the wilderness as a place of temptation while also the source of transcendence from that temptation is depicted in the life and legend of William of Maleval. A French soldier who renounced his immoral ways and journeyed to Rome, he met with Pope Eugene III, who sent him to Jerusalem to seek penance. William began a life of pilgrimages, bringing him across Italy and making him known as a pious mentor—complicating his desire to live as a hermit. After leading a monastery near Pisa, William tired of the lax monks and headed to the wilderness of Monte Pruno. His disciples followed, so William moved again to the desert valley of Maleval near Siena to seek true solitude. He lived in a cave before staying in a small cabin and ate only "roots and herbs for a year."[73] The one disciple who followed him there, Alberto, documented William's "penances and austerities," which included "hair shirts, prayer, contemplation, and mortification."[74] After William's death in 1157, Alberto and another disciple founded the order of the Hermits of Saint William, which spread across Europe and thrived until the eighteenth century.

Far from an aberration, William of Maleval's life journey—however laced with embellishment and fiction—follows the typology established by John the Baptist's essential role in the biblical narrative, carried forward by the Desert Fathers and splintered in the story of the wild man of the forest. John is the ultimate link between the Old and New Testament conception of the wilderness; he is not only wild in body, but his way of life is also radically wild, and he remains on the periphery of tradition, a prototypical Christ.

John's relationship with Jesus reveals how the wilderness transformed from a place of prophecy to a fount of salvation. John's baptism of Jesus in the Jordan River is Jesus's "first appearance on the stage of history as an adult."[75] Once he is raised from the water, the Holy Spirit descends upon him, and "a voice came from the heavens, 'You are my beloved Son; with you I am well pleased.'"[76] Jesus is held in John's arms when he is first publicly heralded as the Son of God. In Mark's Gospel, this announcement is immediately followed by the Holy Spirit driving Jesus into the desert wilderness, where he remains for forty days and fasts while "tempted by Satan."[77] He rejects the temptations of power—with the mountainous and arid expanse of the wilderness as a dramatic backdrop, both exposing him to temptation and steeling him in faith.

A man formed by the wilderness baptizes Jesus, who then goes to the wilderness himself, where he is tested. When Jesus returns from the wilderness and travels to Caesarea Philippi with his disciples, he asks of them, "Who do people say that I am?"[78] Their first reply is John the Baptist, and then Elijah. The prophetic story is most linear in Mark's Gospel. Isaiah's prediction of "a wilderness herald" is followed by John's appearance in the wilderness. His "clothing and food authenticate him as that wilderness herald," and then Jesus is baptized, then tempted in the wilderness—and upon his return, his identity is wedded to these wilderness predecessors.[79] Although John might have been considered a "marginal" Jew in his time, the wilderness itself was a centering place for story and belief.

Jesus's spiritual formation through the wilderness—and therefore through John—makes both theological and practical sense. Their ministries certainly differed in important ways. John's "need to have abundant water at hand for numerous baptisms, his own ascetic diet of locusts and wild honey, and perhaps his jaundiced view of what was going on in the Jerusalem temple, all kept him within a restricted area and thus kept him from a wide-ranging, all-inclusive mission."[80] Those who sought baptisms—including Jesus—traveled to John. Jesus, though, "undertook an itinerant mission"[81] with a focus "on the good news of God's kingly rule, already powerfully at work in Jesus' healings and exorcisms, as well as in his welcome and table fellowship extended to sinners and toll collectors."[82]

Yet Jesus could never truly be seen as "without John," for he "carried John's eschatology, concern for a sinful Israel facing God's imminent judgement, call to repentance, and baptism with him throughout his own ministry."[83] His desert temptation had even earlier parallels. Jesus in the desert could be seen as a "second Adam in the wilderness," one who "had reversed the consequences of Adam's temptation in Paradise, in conformity perhaps also with the ideal of the steadfast martyr surrounded in the sands of the arena by hostile beasts."[84] The wilderness was outside the borders of civilization, but it has always been home to faith—and that home is often where belief is most tested and sustained.

1

Tempted

God in the Desert

"The soul cannot know God," Abba Ammonas wrote in the fourth century, "unless it withdraws itself from men and from every distraction."[1] Ammonas was a disciple of Saint Anthony the Great, a monk who crossed the Nile to barricade himself within an abandoned military fort on Mount Pispir—now Deir Al-Maymun, Egypt. Snakes and other reptiles scurried upon his arrival. Hunkered down with only patience and prayer, Anthony drove away scores of harassing demons and even faced Satan.

For those like Saint Anthony, Henri Nouwen writes, "solitude is not a private, therapeutic place. Rather, it is the place of conversion, the place where the old self dies and the new self is born, the place where the emergence of the new man and the new woman occurs."[2] The solitude of the open, arid desert is both disorienting and calming: a strain on the body and a stirring of the soul. The wilderness is where God descends and disrupts. Faith is charged there.

Richard Rodriguez explains that "Christianity, like Judaism, like Islam, is a desert religion, an oriental religion, a Semitic religion, born of sinus-clearing glottal consonants, spit, dust, blinding light."[3] He laments that most "occidental Christians" are only aware of Christianity's "westward" shift "to Antioch, to Rome, to Geneva, to the pale foreheads of Thomistic philosophers, to Renaissance paintings, to glitter among the frosts of English Christmas cards."[4] Christianity was displaced from its original setting.

Drawn to a passage from Second Maccabees—"The Lord, however, had not chosen the people for the sake of the Place, but the Place for the sake of the people"—Rodriguez concludes that "God happened upon Abraham. Abraham is the desert."[5] In the desert, we feel "a sense of rebuff and contest with the natural world."[6] Rodriguez finds "a system of metaphor and a pervading sense of the irony" in that the Israelites, the chosen people, came from the "desert floor," where living becomes "an unending test of endurance. For all the humiliations the desert inflicted upon them, however, it was from the desert that all the Israelites projected, also, an imagination of the metaphysical world."[7] The ultimate spread of Christianity to town and terrace, however welcomed by the faithful, risks the loss of cultivating context. The further that belief moves from its land of origin, the further it risks being made sentimental, trite, and domesticated. Its roughness and even its strangeness risk becoming neutered in favor of a revised faith born not of desert gales but of gentle breezes that sneak into open windows.

The biblical desert is a proving ground for believers whose bodies are blared by heat and wind. In the desert of Paran, God guided the Israelites "through the vast and terrible wilderness with its saraph serpents and scorpions, its parched and waterless ground; he brought forth water for you from the flinty rock and fed you in the wilderness with manna, a food unknown to your ancestors, that he might afflict you and test you, but also make you prosperous in the end."[8]

Tested and afflicted, those marked by that desert wilderness soon learned that "no amount of skill and discipline will guarantee survival, so desert life requires that people help each other," leading to "more direct trust in God."[9] The desert enables rejuvenation and revelation: there, people "hear the voice of God more clearly, unimpeded by civilization or their own rationalizations."[10]

The voice of John the Baptist cries out from that wilderness, a path later followed by Jesus. He "was led by the Spirit into the desert to be tempted by the devil. He fasted for forty days and forty nights, and afterwards he was hungry," creating a precedent that would be followed by the Desert Fathers and Mothers.[11] Among "wild beasts," Jesus was ministered to by angels.[12] Forged by that time in the desert, Jesus would return there during moments of particular strife.[13] After learning of John the Baptist's execution, Jesus "withdrew in a boat to a deserted place by himself."[14] When the crowd observes the miracle of the loaves and fishes, they identify Jesus as "the Prophet, the one who is to come into the world."[15] Jesus then "withdrew again to the mountain alone."[16]

The Desert Fathers and Mothers would embrace that tradition of wilderness renewal. These Christians, Thomas Merton thought, were not only "heirs to the vocation of the martyrs, but the martyrs are the heirs of those pre-desert fathers, the prophets."[17] Merton, one of our finest modern writers of spiritual longing, was particularly drawn to these desert pilgrims. Even at Gethsemani, his Trappist monastery in Kentucky, Merton felt the pull to plunge into nature. His forest experiences there were certainly transformative, but Merton desired a purer asceticism: the type brought on by climate that pushes bodies to their brinks. Merton needed the desert, and when he could not go there, he needed the stories that came from the desert.

"Once the persecutions of Christians ended," Nouwen reflects, "it was no longer possible to witness for Christ by following him as a blood witness."[18] These monks saw their pilgrimage to the desert as "the way to escape a tempting conformity to the world."[19] They were suspicious of any purported "Christian state," doubting "that Christianity and politics could ever be mixed to such an extent as to produce a fully Christian society."[20] Nouwen shares the example of Abba Arsenius, who heard a voice telling him to "flee, be silent, pray always, for these are the sources of sinlessness."[21] Flee, be silent, and pray together offer a refrain for how the desert prevents "the world from shaping us in its image and are thus the three ways to life in the Spirit."[22]

Unsatisfied with "arguments, concepts and technical verbiage" about God, those who flocked to the desert sought faith through fire.[23] Their journey to the wilderness meant submerging "in the inner, hidden reality of a self that was transcendent, mysterious, half-known, and lost in Christ."[24] Yet as Merton knew, these Christian pilgrims were not ecstatics. The hagiographies of their lives—so common in the folkloric narratives of saints—caused some to mistakenly ascribe a "reputation for fanaticism" to these desert Christians.[25] Rather, they "were humble, quiet, sensible people, with a deep understanding of human nature and enough understanding of the things of God to realize that they knew very little about Him."[26]

Merton preferred the Latin sayings of these Christians, collected in *Verba seniorum*, but all of the writings of the Desert Fathers tended to be plain, terse, and aphoristic rather than ornate, wrought, and stylistic. While Egypt was "seething with religious and intellectual controversies," the desert offered another option: a good reason "for them to keep their mouths shut."[27] They embraced silence, and they embraced work. They used palm leaves and reeds to weave baskets and mats to be sold in towns that bordered the desert.[28]

Most importantly, they prayed. Contemplation and psalmody—vocal "recitation of the Psalms and other parts of the Scriptures which everyone had to know by heart"—were at the center of their prayer.[29] They sought "unceasing prayer," captured in the Greek word *hesychia*: to come to rest.[30] Merton became enraptured with their methods and wondered, "Could I end up as something of a hermit-priest, of a priest of the woods or the deserts or the hills, devoted to a Mass of pure adoration that would put all nature on my paten in the morning and praise God more explicitly with the birds?"[31]

For Merton, the Desert Fathers were the perfect synthesis of untouchable past and present inspiration. "In our day," he lamented, "when 'the world' is everywhere, even in the desert where it makes and proves its secret weapons, the solitary retains his unique and mysterious function."[32] When his "whole being was full of serenity and vigilance"[33] after reading the stories of these desert Christians, Merton was most emboldened to be "on our guard against our natural obsession with the visible, social and communal forms of Christian life which tend at times to be inordinately active, and often become deeply involved in the life of secular, non-Christian society."[34] The desert was kenotic for these early Christians; it required an "arid, rugged purification of the heart."[35] In fact, Merton looked back to Genesis itself, saying that the Desert Fathers sought the renewal of a "lost innocence, the emptiness and purity of heart which had belonged to Adam and Eve in Eden."[36]

Those are grand proclamations by a sentimental storyteller, but they are not without merit. Merton was attracted to the lives and lines of the Desert Fathers for good reason. Their collected sayings, both spare and senseful, feel equally steeped in ambiguity and context. Perhaps it is a trick or miracle of the desert that their laconic anecdotes feel eerily contemporary and prescient.

The Desert Fathers, above all other elements, found power in the solitude of the desert. Eucherius of Lyons surmised that "although God is present everywhere, and regards the whole world as his domain, we may believe that his preferred place is the solitudes of heaven and of the desert."[37] For Abba Andrew, the three things most appropriate for a monk were "exile, poverty, and endurance in silence."[38] Abba Netras, who later became bishop of Pharan, told a disciple that while he was in a cell on Mount Sinai, he attended to his bodily needs more generously than when he returned to civilization. While in the desert, he explained, "[I] had interior peace and poverty and I wished to manage my body, so as not to be ill and not need what I did not have."[39]

Solitude, in the words of Nouwen, "is the furnace of transformation."[40] Solitude, though, could become sinful. Abba John of Diolcos warned that solitude for its own sake created men who "become so savage due to the unbroken silence of the desert" that they hate any vestiges of society, including community.[41] Basil of Caesarea criticized those who seek absolute solitude rather than service as being less than Christlike: "Whose feet then will you wash?"[42]

Asceticism, particularly in the desert, could become its own cult. Here the tendency toward supernatural hagiography can make the desert Christians indistinguishable from secular folklore. The practical rewards of desert faith, therefore, become supplanted with heroic fiction, crafted for plot rather than piety. In reality, the Desert Fathers realized that asceticism was not its own end; they were not engaged in athletic and spiritual competition with each other. Here Merton is again attuned to his predecessors. An asceticism, desert or otherwise, that makes us "odious to ourselves" and that makes "all pleasure seem gross and disgusting" is ultimately a "perversion of the nature which God made good and which even sin has not succeeded in rendering totally vile."[43] Instead, the desert was "a return to fidelity, to charity, to fraternal union; it meant the destruction of the inequalities and oppressions dividing rich and poor."[44] The desert compelled believers to embrace the Sabbath, since "the law of the desert was the law of the Sabbath, of peace, direct dependence on the Lord, silence and trust, forgiveness of debts, restoration of unity, purity of worship."[45] This desert-borne purity is not quite innocence. It is a hard-won "quintessentially pure love of self."[46]

The prototypical desert-ascetic is Saint Anthony, and his life and legend offer an explanation for why the wilderness of the desert cultivates belief. Born in Egypt in 251, he embraced an ascetic life shortly after his teens, discarding the inheritance he received from his deceased parents after hearing Jesus's admonition spoken at church: "If you wish to be perfect, go, sell what you have and give to [the] poor, and you will have treasure in heaven. Then come, follow me."[47] According to his disciple Athanasius, whose *Life of Antony* became the template for monastic biographies, Anthony wished to leave society. He thrust himself into a life of prayer, making him the perfect target for the devil.

The devil tempted Anthony, much as he had done before in the desert with Christ. In response, Anthony "practiced the 'weighing' of his 'thoughts,' a technique of introspection that enabled him to attend to, without being seduced by, the flood of feelings and memories that might divert him from his single-minded purpose."[48] He ate once a day. Or he ate once every two or four days. Only bread, salt, and water. He often slept on the dirt. He banished desires along with idle thoughts. He was getting closer to his spirit: mentally and physically.

The devil continued to prod Anthony with bread, with perversions of Scripture, with empty promises. The monk never relented, and his witness and influence led Athanasius to voice his famous line: "And so, from then on, there were monasteries in the mountains, and the desert was made a city by monks, who left their own people and registered themselves for the citizenship in the heavens."[49]

Anthony's life influenced countless Christians as well as secular artists and writers—perhaps none more than Gustave Flaubert, the French novelist. The author of *Madame Bovary* might seem like an unlikely devotee of a fourth-century anchorite, but their connection speaks volumes about the paradoxes of influence. While in Genoa, Italy, in 1845, Flaubert saw Pieter Breughel's mystical painting of Saint Anthony and was transfixed by the ascetic's peculiar life.[50] *The Temptation of Saint Anthony*, Flaubert's own novel-play, is a masterpiece, a menagerie, one of the most fascinating works of religiously inspired fiction.

Flaubert called the book "the work of my entire life."[51] Charles Baudelaire described it as "the secret chamber of Flaubert's mind."[52] He started the novel shortly after his Genoa trip and would publish its final version in 1874. The essential English translation of the work was completed by Lafcadio Hearn, a Jesuit-schooled writer who, while a schoolboy, "confessed to a priest the hope that a temptress would come to him as she had to the anchorites in the desert."[53]

God-haunted, with an eye on evil, Hearn was the perfect man for the job. Flaubert's novel is dizzying, delusional, groundbreaking. His setting is inspired by "Anthony's final mountain retreat—which Athanasius says has a few old palm trees, and where the saint spent his time praying and weaving mats—mixed with elements of the retreat on Mount Pispir."[54] Flaubert's soul had been stirred by the painting, but the monk had been on his mind for years. The philosopher Michel Foucault, a great admirer of the novel, notes that "as a child, Flaubert saw *The Mystery of Saint Anthony* performed numerous times by Père Legrain in his puppet theater; he later brought George Sand to a performance."[55] The inherent strangeness of puppetry—absurdity bobbing along in front of us—was a curiously apt vehicle for Anthony's unusual life.

Flaubert was nearly ecstatic while writing the book: "I spend my afternoons with the shutters closed, the curtains drawn, and without a shirt, dressed as a carpenter. I bawl out! I sweat! It's superb. . . . I have never been more excited."[56] Foucault thought the book unlocks all of Flaubert's other works: "Standing alongside his other books, standing behind them, the *Temptation* forms a prodigious reserve: for scenes of violence, phantasmagoria, chimeras, nightmares, slapstick."[57] In fact, Flaubert consumed an encyclopedic scope of religious, philosophical, literary, and cultural sources for the book—it was as if he was trying to fit all of human experience into a single allegorical tale.

The novel "takes the form of a theatrical presentation: the transcription of a text that is not meant to be read, but recited and staged."[58] It is a secular liturgy, a performance on the page that requires the reader's deep attention and participation. The novel is, perhaps in spite of Flaubert's own religious agnosticism, a devotional work—a writer's obsessive, lifelong devotion to a story anchored in a spiritual battle in the desert.

In the book, Anthony's mountaintop cabin is made from "mud and reeds" and is "flat-footed and doorless."[59] Inside, there is some water and bread, along with remnants of Anthony's basket weavings. About ten paces from the cabin is "a long cross planted in the soil."[60] Anthony is described as having a "long beard" and "long hair" and as wearing "a tunic of goatskin."[61] He sits cross-legged and is weaving, his mind drifting from work to sky and back to work.

He sees "a flock of birds pass, forming a triangular battalion, gleaming like one sheet of metal, of which the edges alone seem to quiver."[62] Anthony thinks, "How I should like to follow them!"[63]

Flaubert's vision of Anthony begins with such lamentations: the hope that these burdens might pass from him.

They do not. Flaubert begins a thunderous sequence of horrors, hallucinations, and perversions that last for the entire book. Anthony's experiences are unlike the spare aphoristic words of the Desert Fathers: he shakes, he suffers, he nearly sins. Flaubert's novel is an exhaustive and exhausting work—the reader is left disoriented. In all ways textual and experiential, Flaubert succeeds in offering an authentic representation of desert asceticism at its most enthralling.

Flaubert's scenes of Anthony's hallucinations are hellish. In one, Anthony travels to the court of King Nebuchadnezzar. There, "on the pavement below crawl the captive kings whose hands and feet have been cut off; from time to time he flings them bones to gnaw."[64] Below them, "from the depths of the ergastula arise moans of ceaseless pain. Sweet slow sounds of a hydraulic organ alternate with choruses of song."[65] After these visions, Anthony whips himself using "a bunch of thongs with metallic hooks attached to their ends," his shirt off, looking toward heaven.[66]

Hilarion, a disciple of Anthony, asks the monk dogmatic questions to unnerve him: "Why did he receive the Holy Spirit, being himself Son of the Holy Spirit? What need had he of baptism if he was the Word? How could the Devil have tempted him, inasmuch as he was God? Have these thoughts never occurred to thee?"[67] In this and other scenes, we might imagine Flaubert pacing to and fro in his small room, suffused with a torrent of doubt and faith that comes from living with a story for decades.

Late in the novel, the devil appears in body to Anthony and shows him the cosmological wonders of the universe—seeking to distance him from his humble relationship with God through the temptation of knowledge. Undaunted, Saint Anthony resists, but the devil grabs the monk and, "holding him at arms' length, glares at him with mouth yawning as though to devour him."[68] The devil says, "Adore me, then!—and curse the phantom thou callst God!" Anthony rejects him, and the devil leaves.[69]

At the end of the novel, "clouds of gold uprolling in broad volutes unveil the sky."[70] Anthony sees the face of Christ in the sun. The monk "makes the sign of the cross, and resumes his devotions."[71] The unceasing dark theater of the story is replaced by Anthony's true purpose and focus: God.

Merton cautions that the real Saint Anthony is not this novelistic saint. The real monk, Merton acknowledged, "attained apatheia after long and somewhat spectacular contests with demons. But in the end he concluded that not even the devil was purely evil, since God could not create evil, and all His works are good."[72] Flaubert's vision is more haunting than Merton's conception, and yet both can exist. The desert's ability to viscerally transform us, body and soul, means faith can take many forms. Anthony's ability to transcend dogmatic adherence, though, is telling. Flaubert's hagiographic fiction affirms the power of the ascetic moment. If we follow Flaubert's structural arrangement to its conclusion, then Anthony's emotional bareness on a bare mountain does feel like a performance.

Although Merton admired Anthony, he perhaps had even more affinity for Saint John Climacus. Born in the sixth century in Constantinople, Climacus existed in the mold of Anthony but somehow felt more contemporary to Merton. His great spiritual work *The Holy Ladder* "is a tough, hard-hitting, merciless book. Climacus was a kind of sixth-century desert Hemingway."[73] Unlike the original Desert Fathers, who "were silent, humble men who seemed unable to say anything except in the fewest possible words," Climacus was a prose stylist.[74] In the first ladder of his ascent, the renunciation of life, Climacus writes that violence and "unending pain are the lot of those who aim to ascend to heaven with the body, and this especially at the early stages of the enterprise, when our pleasure-loving disposition and our unfeeling hearts must travel through overwhelming grief toward the love of God and holiness." As if to capture the breath of his resigned reader, Climacus writes, "It is hard, truly hard. There has to be an abundance of invisible bitterness, especially for the careless, until our mind, that cur sniffing around the meat market and reveling in the uproar, is brought through simplicity, deep freedom from anger and diligence to a love of holiness and guidance."[75] *The Holy Ladder* portrays the "spiritual life" as a "holy war, a death struggle with the devil, in which one must kill or be killed."[76] God is distant and detached, and no simple penance is enough to achieve divine mercy.

Similarly, the Gospel vision of the desert is a place of endurance, of prayer—preparation for what would come. Christ suffered in the desert as he would in the garden of Gethsemane, a scene that served as the "exemplar and meritorious cause of the charity of all the martyrs and all the hermits who would be tested, like Christ himself, in the furnace of tribulation because they were pleasing to God."[77]

God happened upon Abraham, and Abraham is in the desert—so if we are to follow Rodriguez's formulation, then God and the desert are intertwined. The land, the wind, the sky: it is divine. Desert temptations often came from perversions of the self; open and revealed, the desert believer had only their own body to battle. The desert is the preternatural wilderness of faith: a prototype that would later be repeated, reversed, and revised in prayer, in life, and in story.

2

Wild Creativity
Gerard Manley Hopkins

"Christ tempted in the wilderness," Gerard Manley Hopkins wrote in his notebook in March 1884.[1] The British Jesuit priest had arrived in Dublin a month earlier. A Fellow in Classics, he would soon grade over a thousand Latin and Greek degree examinations in addition to his preparation and papers for the courses he taught. After several years of such arduous work, he suffered in body and soul. He was exhausted. Disillusioned. "Five wasted years have passed in Ireland. I am ashamed of the little I have done, of my waste of time, although my helplessness and weakness is such that I could scarcely do otherwise . . . but what is life without aim, without spur, without help?"[2]

That help, for Hopkins, could only come from Christ. "Pray to be guided by the Holy Ghost in everything," the priest wrote. "Consider that he was now led to be tempted and the field and arena of the struggle was a wilderness, where the struggle wd. be intenser but not perhaps more perilous, to a fallen man, as Satan might suppose him to be. Here admire our Lord in his struggle and his servants St. Antony, St. Cuthbert, and others."[3]

For Saint Anthony, the wilderness was the desert; for Hopkins, the present wilderness was his dark, unforgiving city. Yet there was another deeper sense of wilderness for Hopkins: a place not of pain and suffering but of rejuvenation and resurrection. Despite his reputation as a lackluster preacher, an uninspiring teacher, and an eccentric priest, Hopkins was a radically gifted poet of unparalleled vision—and his poetic gifts came from that vision of wilderness.

Hopkins viewed the wilderness as a free, raw place teeming with weeds and trees and water. A place where souls like his could wander and get lost within—but never hurt. If we are lucky and sensitive enough (Hopkins suggested in his poetry, journals, and letters), the wilderness is a place that could reciprocate its transformative powers and invite us into divine communion.

The wilderness was the God-created world in all of its purity and strangeness—creation unbridled. The perfect fodder for a poet who sought to stretch language to capture the ineffable and channel the Holy Spirit. Never staid, always surprising, the wilderness revealed to Hopkins that something ancient is not unchanging; it is both material and metaphor for Christ, who Hopkins envisioned as a transcendent spirit whose incarnation revealed truth.

Born in 1844, Hopkins was raised in the High Church Anglican tradition. A dynamic student, he excelled at Balliol College, Oxford—and converted to Catholicism in 1866. He was received into the church by another convert, John Henry Newman. In 1868, when the ardent but nervous Hopkins entered the Society of Jesus as a priest, Newman congratulated him with a note: "Don't call the 'Jesuit discipline hard,' it will bring you to heaven."[4]

His first stroke of discipline was a rejection of self: he burned his poems. Some, pieced together through his surviving notebooks, survived the pyre—including the Oxford-composed "The Alchemist in the City." The poem begins with a description of changing nature compared to the narrator's stillness: "My window shows the travelling clouds, / Leaves spent, new seasons, alter'd sky, / The making and the melting crowds: / The whole world passes: I stand by."[5] Later in the poem appear lines that speak to Hopkins's poetic soul and view of the world: "I desire the wilderness / Or weeded landslips of the shore."[6]

In 1863, upon entry at Oxford, Hopkins wrote a letter detailing his wild soul: "I have particular periods of admiration for particular things in Nature; for a certain time I am astonished at the beauty of a tree, shape, effect, etc., then when the passion, so to speak, has subsided, it is consigned to my treasury of explored beauty, while something new takes its place in my enthusiasm."[7]

His Oxford diary is rife with paeans to wilderness. Hopkins would often go on walks with friends and then afterward document the sights and sounds. He was taken with similes: not for novelty but to suggest intersections of worlds. "A plain lies on the opposite side to Oxford with villages crowned with square church-towers shining white here and there," he wrote after an April 1864 stroll. "The lines of the fields, level over level, are striking, like threads in a loom."[8] That night, "moonlight" was "hanging or dropping on treetops like blue cobweb."[9] The next month, he was particularly attuned to surrounding melodies: "Peewits wheeling and tumbling, just as they are said to do, as if with a broken wing. They pronounce *peewit* pretty distinctly, sometimes querulously, with a slight metallic tone like a bat's cry."[10]

These were not merely stray observations. Hopkins specifically labeled them as "notes for poetry."[11] Terse but textured, these notes were collected and cultivated. A March 1865 note—"Feathery rows of young corn. Ruddy, furred and branchy tops of the elms backed by rolling cloud"—is the type of fodder that would make "The Alchemist in the City" possible.[12] Hopkins was especially drawn to trees. Multiple and yet singular, grand and yet fragile, they were full of paradoxes. Trees had bodies, and even before Hopkins's ascetic turn as a Jesuit, he was drawn to the Catholic tendency to view the body as a beautiful, complex image of God. "Vermilion look of the hand held against a candle," he wrote in 1866, "with the darker parts as the middles of the fingers and especially the knuckles covered with ash."[13] He would return to this sense of nature as an extension and expression of his body. A year later, while lying in the grass at Oxford, he put his hand up to block the sun and "saw more richness and beauty in the blue than I had known of before, not brilliance but glow and colour. It was not transparent and sapphire-like, but turquoise-like, swarming and blushing round the edge of the hand and in the pieces clipped in by the fingers, the flesh being sometimes sunlit, sometimes glassy with reflected light, sometimes lightly shadowed in that violet one makes with cobalt and Indian red."[14]

Hopkins was beginning to notice a trend. He was attracted to tension. He was drawn to structure. He loved the wild world, but he sought to appreciate it from the inside. He began to cultivate a theory that might give flesh to his sense of the natural world. Shortly after his graduation from Oxford in 1867, Hopkins compiled notes on Parmenides, the ancient Greek philosopher and poet who sought to understand the nature of reality. Hopkins summarizes the thinker's central argument to mean "that all things are upheld by instress and are meaningless without it."[15] The term *instress* is used as a close corollary to another term in his notes, *inscape*, a concept often related to "proportion."[16] By "proportion," Hopkins means that inscape is the unique and distinct element of a thing. Instress is what *holds* everything together, and instress also enables us to see, understand, and appreciate something.

This is the start of a theory, not a completed treatise. His conception of inscape would soon evolve, splinter, and unify again. It would be ambiguous and odd and perhaps only clear to Hopkins himself. Yet the concept of inscape defines the way that Hopkins understands both the wilderness of nature as well as the wilderness of poetry. Inscape appears regularly in his journal around the time he burns his poems and swears off new verse. Inscape is Hopkins's personal song, his poetry without poems. Inscape was Hopkins's attempt to quantify the sublimity of the wild: to capture, in verse, that intangible feeling of being stirred by nature, the moments when we are convinced the wild is part of a grand divine plan.

Before he entered the Jesuit novitiate at Manresa, Roehampton, Hopkins spent a month in Switzerland. His burnt poems were fresh in his mind, but the open air afforded him new inspiration. He found inscape everywhere: in trees, in plants, and among the mountain pastures. He traveled to Grindelwald, where he saw brooks slanted and falling so that the glaciers were "cross-hatched with their crevasses but they form waves which lie regularly and in horizontals across the current," leading him to comment that the water had a "real inscape."[17]

Inscape could be used to describe the symmetry of trees, the flow of waters, and the mountains themselves, like the ranges at Zermatt, which were "concave, cusped; they run like waves in the wind, ricked and sharply inscaped."[18] Hopkins traveled down the Rhone valley to a small Catholic section in Visp, where he enjoyed Spanish chestnuts, "their inscape here bold, jutty, somewhat oak-like, attractive, the branching visible and the leaved peaks spotted so as to make crests of eyes."[19] Toward the end of his holiday, sick in his room, Hopkins saw "a slender race of fine flue cloud inscaped in continuous eyebrow curves hitched on the Weisshorn peak as it passed."[20] Inscape seemed like Hopkins's attempt to capture existence itself: beauty, perhaps.

He would later describe inscape as "design, pattern"—that which "I above all aim at in poetry."[21] But for now, Hopkins was firmly ensconced in his Jesuit studies, a nearly decade-long journey of philosophy, theology, and teaching. Although he was not writing poems, he was inhaling nature and cultivating a sense of wonder in the wilderness. That sense compelled him to continually see the natural world anew, as he did with a sunset in March of 1870. The sky was beautiful: the "dead clear blue" above, the sundown "yellow, moist with light."[22] Of particular interest, though, was that Hopkins pondered how when we often view a sunset, our eyes are wounded by the sun—so we must cover the origin of the light to experience the light itself. Yet "today I inscaped them together and made the sun the true eye and ace of the whole, as it is. It was all active and tossing out light and started as strongly forward from the field as a long stone or a boss in the knop of the chalice-stem; it is indeed by stalling it so that it falls into scape with the sky."[23]

Inscape is then not only a way of attempting to describe the internal elements of nature. It is a way of seeing nature—an active, spiritual communion with the wild. Hopkins often implies that nature is sentient, aware of being seen: "What you look hard at seems to look hard at you, hence the true and the false instress of nature."[24] He watched how chestnut trees "plunged and crossed one another without losing their inscape" yet added a curious parenthetical note: "(Observe that motion multiplies inscape only when inscape is discovered, otherwise it disfigures.)"[25] Inscape and instress of nature compelled Hopkins to look, ponder, question, and document the wilderness. He not only needed to see, but he needed to see often: "Unless you refresh the mind from time to time you cannot always remember or believe how deep the inscape in things is."[26]

In 1871, during his intensive philosophy studies at Saint Mary's Hall of Stonyhurst College in Lancashire, Hopkins made an afternoon visit to Netley Abbey, a Cistercian monastery. He walked among the ruins, appreciating the ivy vines and ash trees as well as how even the dew held "the bright pieces of evening light."[27] He stopped to appreciate one dead tree in particular, and his observations show how inscape and instress relate to each other: "the inscape markedly holding its most simple and beautiful oneness up from the ground through a graceful swerve below (I think) the spring of the branches up to the tops of the timber. I saw the inscape freshly, as if my mind were still growing, though with a companion the eye and the ear are for the most part shut and instress cannot come."[28]

Inscape transcended flora and fauna, living and dead. The entire natural world, for Hopkins, was wilderness—and it was a world that filled him with "delightful fear."[29] His gentle fear was a part of his eccentric vision of the world; although any discussion of Hopkins's strangeness and eccentricity is meant in the most positive sense of those terms. For the world itself is wild and strange—and Hopkins was merely more attuned than most to its whispers. Hopkins kept his eyes on creatures great and small, including bats "flying at midday and circling so near that I could see the ears and the claws and the purplish web of the wings with the ribs and veins through it."[30]

On Holy Saturday in 1872, Hopkins described the sky as "warm, with thunder, odd tufts of thin-textured very plump round clouds something like the eggs in an opened ant-hill"—his linking of nature to nature both clarifies each and suggests a synchronicity of existence.[31] Although these observations were documented in his dense, flowing notebook, he still abstained from writing poems. Even a brief note on inscape during this winter period is telling. When Hopkins writes that he "caught an inscape as flowing and well marked almost as the frosting on glass and slabs; but I could not reproduce it afterwards with the pencil," it feels like a gentle admission that the profound beauty of the world that he was able to view remained distant from him in the act of creation.[32]

It took a tragedy—far from him in location but not in spirit—to bring Hopkins back to poetry. On December 7, 1875, a German steamship bound for New York became caught in a blizzard and ran aground. Hopkins was particularly moved by the death of five Franciscan nuns, exiles from Germany who bore witness to their faith until the end. Hopkins finished his long poem based on the tragedy in January 1876 and then continued to write—his regular observations of nature finding form and life in his verse. He was ordained a priest in September 1877, and the poems written during the preceding months are suffused with a piety born of the natural world.

"The world is charged with the grandeur of God," he begins his poem "God's Grandeur."[33] Constructed as a single sentence that ends with the divine, Hopkins leaves no doubt in his pronouncement. This God-gifted world "will flame out," he warns. Hopkins means our natural and organic world, a beautiful and vulnerable wilderness trampled by man: "Generations have trod, have trod, have trod; / And all is seared with trade; bleared, smeared with toil; / And wears man's smudge and shares man's smell: the soil / Is bare now, nor can foot feel, being shod."[34] The lines ooze of metal and machine. His monotonous repetition of "have trod" echoes the trampling of forests, the destruction of wilderness. Hopkins is nearly incredulous in this poem; his poetic exasperation is usually spent proclaiming the magnificence of Christ, but now he laments how the scarred world bears man's dirtying fingerprint. Despite the toiling of the world, "nature is never spent."[35] Hopkins ends with an optimistic vision: "Oh, morning, at the brown brink eastward, springs— / Because the Holy Ghost over the bent / World broods with warm breast and with ah! bright wings."[36] The wilderness is a sacred place: a gift that must be loved and conserved.

Hopkins continues this sacral sense of the wilderness in "Easter." The poem's overall tone is joy; it is written to be read on Easter day. His exhortation to "pluck the harp and breathe the horn" is followed by a question: "Know ye not 'tis Easter morn?"[37] Hopkins suggests that we might be unaware of the power of the resurrection, and we might learn gratitude from the wilderness: "Gather gladness from the skies; / Take a lesson from the ground; / Flowers do ope their heavenward eyes."[38] The wilderness, being a product of creation, is compelled toward the creator—a logical route, Hopkins implies, that humans should follow.

Hopkins regularly associates wildness with nature in its truest form. The beauty of the natural world comes from being unbound, as in "Spring," a poem praising the season when "weeds, in wheels, shoot long and lovely and lush."[39] Wilderness is this wildness: the overgrown world worthy of praise. "Glory be to God for dappled things," Hopkins writes in "Pied Beauty," its first line a complete sentence, echoing the assured pronouncement of "God's Grandeur."[40] He praises "skies of couple-colour as a brinded cow"—nature (animals) again used to capture the unique state of nature (atmosphere). Pied, dappled, brinded: Hopkins sings of spotted, marked things. He lauds "all things counter, original, spare, strange."[41] These strange things are the finest of creation, for they have not been corrected according to human sense and reason. Hopkins does not claim to understand the peculiarities of the world—as with his parenthetical "(who knows how?)."[42] No matter: when we praise the wilderness, we praise God.

Clever and cunning, Hopkins works wonders with syntax. His praise of nature is explicitly a praise of God, for God creates all. And if all creation is God made, then all iterations and deviations are beautiful. The spare, the strange, the fickle: Hopkins loved them all. "No doubt my poetry errs on the side of oddness," Hopkins admitted in a letter to his friend Robert Bridges—the future poet laureate of England.[43] This oddity was inevitable: perhaps heaven-sent. Hopkins explained that "it is the virtue of design, pattern, or inscape to be distinctive and it is the vice of distinctiveness to become queer."[44] Strangeness was his poetic destiny: "Every true poet . . . must be original and originality a condition of poetic genius; so that each poet is like a species in nature . . . and can never recur."[45] A radical poetic sense was only worthwhile in service of the inscape and divinity he sought to praise.

Hopkins felt an absolute connection with the world, a spirit that sustains poems like "Binsey Poplars." The narrator's lovely trees, whose leaves caught the sun, have been cut down. "My aspens dear, whose airy cages quelled, / Quelled or quenched in leaves the leaping sun," are now gone.[46] "Not spared, not one." He laments, "O if we but knew what we do / When we delve or hew— / Hack and rack the growing green!"[47] His threnody is for the death of the tree, the folly of human intervention ("Where we, even where we mean / To mend her we end her"), and the loss of beauty for future generations ("After-comers cannot guess the beauty been.").[48] The wound was one Hopkins had felt himself. Years earlier, he described an ash tree in the garden that was "lopped": "I heard the sound and looking out and seeing it maimed there came at the moment a great pang and I wished to die and not to see the inscapes of the world destroyed any more."[49]

Perhaps that sharp pain led Hopkins to celebrate and preserve the wilderness in his verse. That celebration occurred in several different modes. In some poems, like "Hurrahing in Harvest," the natural world is an extension of the body. In this poem, summer is over, and "I walk, I lift up, I lift up heart, eyes."[50] This unity is a function of inscape, the recognition that our varied forms contain similar symmetries: "These things, these things were here and but the beholder / Wanting; which two when they once meet, / The heart rears wings bold and bolder / And hurls for him, O half hurls earth for him under his feet."[51] The world, being seen, affirms the viewer.

In "Harry Ploughman," a worker in the fields is described as imbued with the physicality of those fields. The poem is an agile, deft piece of syntax, one of the finest representations of Hopkins's inscape made literal on the page: "Hard as hurdle arms, with a broth of goldish flue / Breathed round; the rack of ribs; the scooped flank; lank / Rope-over thigh; knee-nave; and barreled shank—."[52] This literal inscape makes the poem appear strange at first glance, as inscape here might be considered the "inward fusion of thought and feeling" represented by the "outward harmony of rhythm and sound texture."[53]

The more Harry works the ground, the more he becomes one with the earth. When Hopkins describes Harry at work—"He leans to it, Harry bends, look. Back, elbow, and liquid waist / In him, all quail to the wallowing o' the plough"—his language is meant to be representational, not relational.[54] He wants the texture of his words to capture the mystical sense of the person being described. Hopkins truly held a wilderness vision of language itself.

Poems like "The May Magnificat" imply a divinity to natural growth. Hopkins again returns to spring as a theme of new life and unabashed growth. The narrator asks of the Virgin Mary, "What is Spring?" and she replies, "Growth in every thing— // Flesh and fleece, fur and feather, / Grass and greenworld all together."[55] The blessed mother and nature are one in this season: "All things rising, all things sizing / Mary sees, sympathising / With that world of good, / Nature's motherhood."[56] He continues this vision in another poem about Mary, "The Blessed Virgin Compared to the Air We Breathe." To understand Hopkins, we must realize how his poetry strives to capture his one truth: the world is saturated with God. "Wild air, world-mothering air, / Nestling me everywhere," he writes.[57] "I say that we are wound / With mercy round and round / As if with air."[58] In the same way Mary gave life to and cared for Christ, nature sustains us.

Certainly other poets had written of God and praised divine creation. Yet no poet could capture the possessed inscape of God on the page like Hopkins. And that divine sense is best captured in his sequence of poems that praise the wilderness. Hopkins's ability to affirm the raw beauty of nature is unparalleled.

"Lovely the woods, waters, meadows, combes, vales," Hopkins writes in his poem "In the Valley of the Elwy": "All the air things wear that build this world of Wales."[59] The perfection of his natural praise appears in "Inversnaid," a poem that unifies two of his recurring themes: the animated, geometric beauty of water and waves and his appreciation for the forms of horses. His description of a river from 1870 captures how the water was "wild, very full, glossy brown with mud, furrowed in permanent billows."[60] Hopkins describes a particularly choppy and rock-steeped section of the River Hodder as "burly water-backs which heave after heave kept tumbling up from the broken foam and their plump heap turning open in ropes of velvet"—imbuing the river's flow, bends, and contours with a mammalian body.[61]

The synthesis again captures Hopkins's metaphorical impulse to figuratively reveal nature *through* nature, a deft way to reveal how the natural world was synchronous. In 1874, Hopkins saw the inscape of a horse that made him think of what Sophocles "had felt and expresses in two choruses of the *Oedipus Coloneus*, running on the likeness of a horse to a breaker, a wave of the sea curling over. I looked at the groin or the flank and saw how the set of the hair symmetrically flowed outwards from it to all parts of the body, so that, following that one may inscape the whole beast very simply."[62]

In "Inversnaid," the river (referred to using the dialect term *burn*) becomes the horse: "Of a pool so pitchblack, fell-frowning, / It rounds and rounds Despair to drowning."[63] Hopkins described the genesis of the poem in a letter to Bridges, how he sought to create "something, if I cd. only seize it, on the decline of wild nature," which later becomes "Inversnaid."[64] The poem originally ended with the lines "And wander in the wilderness; / In the weedy wilderness, / Wander in the wilderness."[65]

Hopkins wished to drift into the sublime wild, thinking that there, he could find God incarnated. Inscape formed his poetic sense because he believed that with enough seeing—with enough faith—the wilderness could transform him: a communion with nature. When Hopkins was describing the water at Hodder Roughs, he reflected that "by watching hard the banks began to sail upstream, the scaping unfolded, the river was all in tumult but not running, only the lateral motions were perceived, and the curls of froth where the waves overlap shaped and turned easily and idly."[66] Hopkins's syntax was winding and complex but never lazy—so consistent with his previous conceptions of inscape, it certainly appears the priest suggests the water was responding to *him* perceiving it.[67]

Hopkins is always in awe of the natural world. He lauds its grandeur, its mystery, its abject beauty. So to place himself within the process of that world should be read as an act not of ego but of humility, as well as of further evidence that his encompassing inscape theory is able to capture the spiritual communion of all beings. In fact, that communion extends to all things God made, as when Hopkins described a snowdrift, how the "sharp nape" is "sometimes broken by slant flutes or channels."[68] He thinks the effect must be caused "when the wind after shaping the drift first has changed and cast waves in the body of the wave itself. All the world is full of inscape and chance left free to act falls into an order as well as a purpose."[69] Inscape is the natural inclination of the world left untouched.

This is not to say that Hopkins thought all of existence was without pain. He was acutely aware of sadness, and those feelings increased as his workload became overbearing. Hopkins was truly neither preacher nor teacher, but his Dublin years led to a darker turn in his poetry. He was no less sure of the love of Christ, but he was less sure of the world. In an 1881 letter to his friend Richard Watson Dixon, Hopkins admitted, "I would gladly live all my life, if it were so to be, in as great or a greater seclusion from the world and be busied only with God."[70]

His melancholy sense of nature and humanity is best captured in his poem "Spring and Fall." The poem is invoked to a "young child," Margaret, who is the silent recipient of the adult narrator's lament. Hopkins composed the poem while serving as a parish priest in Lydiate, England, and occasionally celebrated Mass at Rose Hill, a private home. He was not a successful preacher and, devoid of a "working strength," soon afterward left pastoral work.[71]

We can hear the stress of life in these lines. The poem begins with a question: "Márgarét, áre you gríeving / Over Goldengrove unleaving?"[72] "Spring and Fall" is spoken to young Margaret; her name is mentioned in the first and final lines, folding the poem together. Hopkins, like other poets, often accomplishes that wrapping of word and idea through poetic form and rhyme, but the repetition of her name is a reminder that she is being offered advice.

She is sad because the trees are losing leaves. We want to tell her to get over it, perhaps, so as to not waste her tears on such a trivial thing. But the narrator reserves his tough and honest love for the moment: "Leáves like the things of man, you / With your fresh thoughts care for, can you?"[73]

In the first four lines, Hopkins uses variants of "you" four times, the refrain like a consoling touch on the child's shoulder. "Unleaving" falls into "leaves." A question is followed with another question, though the second is directed more toward the reader, who might be the real subject of this poem. The natural death of nature—how the "worlds of wanwood leafmeal lie" on the ground—causes tears in children, but our adult hearts will be wounded in other ways.[74] As "the heart grows older / It will come to such sights colder," and we will no longer "spare a sigh" at bare trees.[75] Hopkins warns the girl: soon, "you wíll weep and know why."[76] It is telling that in a poem of perhaps the most profound grief—a child's realization that she will grow old and die—Hopkins chooses the decay of nature as the central metaphor. We think of Hopkins mourning the felled tree years earlier: of Hopkins looking at the wilderness and feeling it stare back, somehow, in recognition. Of course he would mourn the wild world.

The wrenching crux of "Spring and Fall" is that Margaret is you and I. The narrator of "Spring and Fall" wants Margaret—wants us—to know that the ultimate melancholy is the awareness of our mortality. Poems about death are legion, but Hopkins's careful construction allows his notes to bounce off the other lines. Second person, when used well, is a wonderful poetic mirror. There is even a touch of inscape here in the communion between narrator and recipient, man and child, poem and reader. The poem's soft rhythms lull readers into accepting the inevitability of its narrative: "It ís the blight man was born for, / It is Margaret you mourn for."[77]

The narrator of "Spring and Fall" is world weary and pained. He is willing to reveal the end of innocence. The poem accumulates toward the heavy conclusion that our truest sadness is the recognition that it is not the falling of leaves that pains us but our own falls, however public or private. And yet we live among those leaves; we inhabit an incarnational world with them, so our grief is collective. Several years later, Hopkins's body and spirit had been worn down from being overworked, his own sense of sadness, and the peculiar tension that his priestly duties and identity strained his ability to praise God in his poetry.

Hopkins wrote his final poem, "To R. B.," on April 22, 1889. He had completed a drawing that day of a local stream from "Lord Massey's domain" in Dublin. It was the day after Easter Sunday, and he had been feeling sick. He held on to the poem for a week and then mailed it to the R. B. invoked in the title: Robert Bridges, his longtime friend. They'd met in 1863 at Oxford and began writing letters to each other in 1865. Despite a few pauses, their correspondence would continue for over twenty years. Bridges later collected and published Hopkins's poems in 1918. The two close friends disagreed often—about Catholicism and poetry—and despite Bridges's tepid preface for Hopkins's collected poems, he deserves credit for the publication of Hopkins's innovative, essential work.

Hopkins is playful, pointed, and proud in his letters to Bridges. After Bridges offered some critical advice for his poem "The Wreck of the Deutschland," about the death of five Franciscan nuns, Hopkins said that his "verse is less to be read than heard."[78] Hopkins's insistence on an aural experience of his poetry might seem contradictory to his persistent embrace of seeing the natural world in all of its particular detail. But receiving poetry through the ear requires silence, contemplation, and focus. "I do not write for the public," Hopkins told Bridges. "You are my public and I hope to convert you."[79] Convert, for Hopkins, held a multitude of meanings—but for Hopkins, all roads led to poetry.

"I am ill to-day, but no matter for that as my spirits are good," Hopkins began his April 29, 1889, letter to his friend.[80] "I believe I enclose a new sonnet. . . . This one is addressed to you."[81] His first phrase—"The fine delight that fathers thought"—speaks to the joy of an idea, implying that a certain feeling comes before the poetic creation.[82]

That gentle arrival becomes a bit sharper with the following words: "the strong / Spur, live and lancing like the blowpipe flame."[83] His sounds move from *f* to *s* to *l*; we might wonder if Hopkins, lost in the terrible reverie of sickness, might have thought of that sound from the flowing stream that he'd sketched that same day.

The inspiration described in the first two lines, Hopkins warns, "breathes once," but that breath is "quenchèd faster than it came."[84] Writers know that feeling: the surge of inspiration, the rush that comes within even a single sentence, phrase, or even word of creation, but it soon disappears. "Nine months she then, nay years, nine years" does that absence of inspiration feel.[85] Hopkins used birth metaphors and language elsewhere: for example, the year before, when he said that a sonnet had been "conceived."[86] But this current gestation is too long and is merely the "widow of an insight" now.[87]

At the sonnet's volta, Hopkins offers his desire: "Sweet fire the sire of muse, my soul needs this; / I want the one rapture of an inspiration."[88] This is the language of conflagration, of abject craving. We should remember that these lines are not whispered into the air. They are invoked to his friend. They are also delivered in measured syntax. This is not the sonnet type of "God's Grandeur," where Hopkins's ebullience pushed against the poem's form. This is creation muted: the wilderness silent from river's rush or wind's rattle. When Hopkins ends his poem with the ironic apology that his "lagging lines," however skilled, might miss "the roll, the rise, the creation," he describes his poetic absence as a "winter world."[89] This is a marked contrast from how the natural world is usually portrayed in his poems as a place of transformation and resurrection. Now in his final poem, the wilderness is closer to the stark place where Christ was tested.

In his editor's preface to Hopkins's collected poems, Bridges said that his friend had two faults of oddity and obscurity. Bridges might sound unkind, but he was merely laying bare his own aesthetics. Hopkins embraced his ecstatic strangeness, aware that oddity was charged with the Holy Spirit—and Bridges, skeptical of Hopkins's faith, would never understand. Bridges showed his love for Hopkins in other ways. At the end of his preface, he says, "It is lamentable that Gerard Hopkins died when, to judge by his latest work, he was beginning to concentrate the force of all his luxuriant experiments in rhythm and diction, and castigate his art into a more reserved style."[90] The poem Bridges describes is likely "To R. B."

"To R. B." was the final poem written by Hopkins. Two weeks later, Hopkins became very sick; he died of typhoid fever in early June. "To R. B." is both a lament and apology for Hopkins's lack of inspiration and creation but accumulates to the ironic conclusion that an explanation of writer's block is itself a poem. A subtle, clever turn—one final whisper from a master.

Gerard Manley Hopkins forever changed English poetry: his sprung rhythm lines captured his charged devotion to God and disrupted Victorian formal modes. Yet inextricable from this faith and his style of poetry is his focus on the beauty of the natural, wild world. His notebooks and sketchbooks are saturated with his contemplations of wilderness, and his poetry channels these obsessions into artistic perfection. For Hopkins, the wild world was a source of joy, surprise, and renewal—thematically connected to the life, death, and resurrection of Christ. Although Hopkins was a gifted poet, he struggled with illness and the cloistered feeling of religious life, so the wilderness became a source of imaginative escape and renewal: a true vision of God's presence in our broken world.

3

Stewards of the Gloriously Indifferent

Wendell Berry and Terry Tempest Williams

Wendell Berry and Terry Tempest Williams are writers with evocative visions of the American wilderness: writers who embrace the contradictions of conservation and development. Williams is a sage of the Utah desert; Berry is formed by Kentucky plains and forests. Both Berry and Williams love the wild world, and yet they and their families have farmed and dug trenches and adapted that world. They have, like so many before them, made their livelihood from that land. "You could say this is a real paradox," Williams acknowledges, "to destroy the land, yet love it at the same time."[1] Both are pragmatic idealists and think a Christian vision of wilderness needs, to borrow a phrase from Thomas Merton, an "ecological conscience."[2]

Merton, in fact, has had a notable impact on both writers. In Williams's breakout book, *Refuge: An Unnatural History of Family and Place*, she writes of her mother's cancer against the backdrop of Utah's Great Salt Lake. In one scene, she sits with her mother in the Abbey of Our Lady of the Holy Trinity, among white-robed monks singing vespers before the encroaching October dusk. Afterward, they walk together outside, and although her mother is increasingly frail, Williams comes to an epiphany: "She was letting go. So was I."[3] In this transcendent scene, Williams gains solace from Merton, quoting him: "Silence is the strength of our interior life. . . . If we fill our lives with silence, then we live in hope."[4]

Merton and Berry have an even more direct connection. They began corresponding in 1967, a few years after Berry and his wife, Tanya, returned to Kentucky from New York City. The couple purchased the Lanes Landing Farm, which they own to this day. Merton and Berry were mutual admirers of the poet Denise Levertov, whose mystical verse prefigured her later conversion to Catholicism. Merton even published several of Berry's haikus in the last issue of *Monks Pond*, the short-lived literary magazine he released at the Abbey of Gethsemani, among his fellow Trappist monks. One poem speaks to an anxiety: "I will never sleep: / the thought of the telephone / ringing in the night."[5]

Both writers carry a wilderness lineage from Merton. "We all proclaim our love and respect for wild nature, and in the same breath we confess our firm attachment to values which inexorably demand the destruction of the last remnant of wildness."[6] In June 1968, a few months before his tragic death, Merton wrote an impassioned plea for wilderness in Dorothy Day's newspaper, the *Catholic Worker*. Merton was at his most lyric when writing about nature, his observations taking on the rhythm and spirit of Hopkins: "Whorled dark profile of a river in snow. A cliff in the fog. And now a dark road straight through a long fresh snow field. Snaggy reaches of snow patter. Claws of mountain and valley. Light shadow or breaking cloud on snow. Swing and reach of long, gaunt, black, white forks."[7] Out in the woods, Merton wrote, "I can think of nothing except God and it is not so much that I think of Him either. I am as aware of Him as of the sun and the clouds and the blue sky and the thin cedar trees."[8]

In "The Wild Places," Merton considers American attitudes toward wilderness, stretching back to the American pioneer mythos. The pioneer is created by the wilderness, and yet he also destroyed that wilderness: "His success as a pioneer depends on his ability to fight the wilderness and win. Victory consists in reducing the wilderness to something else, a farm, a village, a road, a canal, a railway, a mine, a factory, a city—and finally an urban nation."[9] Such victory "was an ascetic triumph over the forces of impulse and of lawless appetite."[10] Merton posits this American dislike of the wilderness as coming from the Puritans, whose biblical interpretation led them to hate the wilderness "as a person, an extension of the Evil One, the Enemy opposed to the spread of the Kingdom of God."[11] He cites *Johnson's Wonder-Working Providence*, a seventeenth-century Puritan text, as including a description of Jesus influencing the Puritans to turn "one of the most hideous, boundless and unknown wildernesses in the world . . . to a well-ordered Commonwealth."[12] Rather than a place from which prophets came and Jesus rejected temptation, the wilderness was a place of fear. The wilderness had to be tamed and trimmed.

Yet there was also a romantic vision of the American wild, one influenced by a different European sense and perspective, in which the "Transcendentalists, above all, reversed the Puritan prejudice against nature, and began to teach that in the forests and mountains, God was nearer than in the cities."[13] The pragmatic idealist

Henry David Thoreau, Merton says, "had enough sense to realize that civilization was necessary and right. But an element of wildness was necessary as a component in civilized life itself."[14] For Merton, "Honesty and authenticity do not depend on complete freedom from contradictions—such freedom is impossible—but on recognizing our self-contradictions and not masking them with bad faith."[15] To visit and experience the wilderness was to know ourselves—and illuminate the best traits of civilization.

Berry embraced that sense of contradiction, that the world can never be neatly broken into wild and domestic parts. Wilderness abounds, is constant, is among us in domestic places. Berry seeks to change our language and conception of wilderness. He thinks "we do not need just the great public wildernesses, but millions of private or semi-private ones."[16] Farms should have wild sections. Wilderness should patch "corners of factory grounds and city lots—places where nature is given a free hand, where no human work is done, where people go only as guests."[17] These pockets of wilderness are "sacred groves—places we respect and leave alone, not because we understand well what goes on there, but because we do not."[18]

Wilderness, for Berry, is not defined by scope or volume; there is no minimum acreage to reach such designation. His definition is inclusive and realistic—and one that has evolved from his own experiences in the wild. "The Unforeseen Wilderness," a 1970 essay that was later collected into a book with photographs by Ralph Eugene Meatyard, offers a useful framing for Berry's sense of wilderness. Berry writes about the evolving wilderness of the Red River Gorge of eastern Kentucky. "The bends and bars and pools of the river are not fore-ordained," Berry cautions, "but are made in response to obstructions and openings"—evidence that the wild will always adapt, even when wounded, to the changing world.[19] He recalls a solo canoe trip on the Upper Gorge one Memorial Day. He struggled and had to turn back around.

That failure was revelatory. Berry had thought he understood the wilderness of the Gorge because he had seen its layout and route on maps. Now he experienced the wild as "a presence that I felt in the roots of my hair and the pit of my stomach"—a force, quite directly, of nature.[20] This failure was a lesson in perspective and in humility. He had to learn from the indifferent wilderness. Without the aid of tools and technology, we must face the wilderness with body and spirit, which results in a curious paradox: we realize not only that our place in the wilderness is slight but also that we have a place at all is reward enough.

Daunted, Berry was also inspired. He wanted to change. As he traveled through the Kentucky woods, he concluded that there was only one way to make peace with the wild: "We begin to feel that we are not simply *in* the wilderness, but that we are *part* of it, moving within it in direct response to it, moving as it requires us to move and as it moves. Our journey has become one of its processes."[21]

We are the wild. There's no other way to survive. Concepts like the "environment," however well meaning, imply border and difference. To designate means to subjugate, which begins a cycle that makes Berry skeptical. He rejects a dualistic view of humans and the environment. We eat, digest, and release the environment; it "doesn't *surround* us—it's part of us. We're *of* it, and it's *of* us, and the relationship is unspeakably intimate."[22] An ecological sense is only possible if we enter into the forest, cross the river, and feel the water over our calves, our heels against the rock and sand.

This is a blue-collar, manual sentiment: one that comes from his years of farming. "If you are going to grow corn," he has said, "you have got to slow down to the speed of corn."[23] He humbly wonders,

"What is the nature of this place? And then: What will nature permit me to do here?"[24] Permission is the key idea here, as Berry wants to avoid damage to nature and himself. Instead, he thinks in terms of communion: "How can I make my work harmonize with the nature of the place?"[25]

"Our culture today is mainly embarrassed about country things"[26]—a not only pleasant, idealistic thought but also one that Berry recognized as perilous even in 1973. Only imagination and art can make wilderness palpable and sacred to the masses. Art gives "an imagery or a language or a story" to "reverence or love or compassion or gratitude" in a way that makes them truly visible in our world.[27]

The spiritual worldview that generates these moments of reverence, love, compassion, and gratitude is a generally Christian one for Berry—although he eschews labels of denomination. He admits, "I am a bad-weather churchgoer. When the weather is good, sometimes when it is only tolerable, I am drawn to the woods on the local hillsides or along the streams."[28] Among his lack of orthodoxy, Berry has developed what he views as a "forest Christian" conception of the world, one best articulated in his essay "Christianity and the Survival of Creation."[29] He thinks in terms not of enclosed church and provincial creeds but of God revealed in the wild. Humanity's destruction of wilderness "is not just bad stewardship, or stupid economics, or a betrayal of family responsibility; it is the most horrid blasphemy."[30] He calls the Bible an "outdoor book" or perhaps a "'hypaethral book,' such as Thoreau talked about—a book open to the sky. It is best read and understood outdoors, and the farther outdoors the better."[31]

Outdoors in the wilderness, "we are confronted everywhere with wonders; we see that the miraculous is not extraordinary but the common mode of existence. It is our daily bread."[32] God is found in those spaces, for God, according to Berry, "is the wildest being in existence. The presence of His spirit in us is our wildness, our oneness with the wilderness of Creation."[33] We experience the divine when we are most open to those encounters with the wild—when we "come into the presence of the unqualified and mysterious formality of Creation."[34]

Those encounters are not always pleasant. Sometimes "we go to be chastened or corrected" in the wilderness.[35] We should not, Berry warns, envision the wilderness as a place of escape from our daily world. If the wild and the domestic overlap, as Berry suggests, then a path into the forest is merely another turn in our daily route, only different because the wilderness affords us a clearer view of God.

Although he calls himself an "amateur poet," Berry captures this vision of the salvific power of regular pilgrimages into the wilderness in his Sabbath poems—pieces drafted on Sundays, dating back to 1979. An early poem in the sequence explains his project: he hears church bells and thinks of how generations before him, lifted by faith, brought God among "field and trodden road."[36] Yet the bells instead send him into the woods: "I leave labor and load, / Take up a different story."[37]

In those woods, away from work and institutional religion, Berry finds a "dark-sourced stream" that is "making sound / In its stepped fall from cup to cup / Of tumbled rocks."[38] There is a touch of Hopkins here, as nature begets nature metaphor. In what might be considered his own form of inscape, Berry often returns to the theme of the wilderness reclaiming itself, an inevitable, almost moral, action: "The field finds its source / in the old forest, in the thicket / that returned to cover it, / in the dark wilderness of its soil, / in the dispensations of the sky, / in our time, in our minds— / the righting of what was done wrong."[39]

Nature's healing "will come in spite of us, after us, / over the graves of its wasters, as it comes / to the forsaken fields."[40] The only creed of the wilderness is transcendence, as "the pattern of its break-ing / involves also, given time, / the pattern of its healing."[41] As Berry has written, "The Bible says the earth is the Lord's, and the deed has *never* been transferred to any of us."[42] The inevitable heal-ing of the wilderness is consistent with Berry's vision of the wild as a permeating, God-present place that challenges humans who are present. Berry is most mystical about this idea in his poetry, where juxtaposition of nature's trauma and resurrection feels most immediate.

By returning to the wild—in whatever context is available or approximate to us—we can be reminded again of its ancient spirit. Often a walk in the woods is all that is needed so that the "shadow of old grace returns."[43] In order for that wildness to remain, we must slow our mowers, ease our development, and change our idea of the wilderness as not a distant swath of land to preserve but a place on which we might gently walk. "And while you work your fields," Berry writes, speaking to farmers like himself, "do not forget the woods. / The woods stands by the field / To measure it."[44]

The wilderness will affirm its place and power soon enough. In one poem, Berry writes of how in "a single motion the river comes and goes," a line of life that often flows unnoticed "as it noses calmly along within its bounds / like the family pig."[45] There will be a day, though, when the river "swiftens, darkens, rises, flows over / its banks, spreading its mirrors out upon / the fields of the valley floor, and then / it is like God's love or sorrow, including / at last all that had been left out."[46] Berry's poem is as beautiful as it is devastating—an apt paradox for wilderness itself.

In a 2018 essay, "Wild and Domestic," Berry returns to that paradox as well as his central claim that we must reconsider how we define the wilderness. In contrast with our typical concep-tion of wild places, the wilderness "is in fact a place of domestic order."[47] Wild things challenge each other, but they do so "within a larger, ultimately mysterious order of interdependence and even cooperation."[48]

Berry calls conservationists to task here, for they "prefer the parks and 'wilderness areas' over the rest of the country," thus unwittingly shrinking the places that might be deemed wilderness and making conventional domestic spaces appear sinful for being mundane.[49] The danger is that we "falsely and impossibly consign Nature to the 'wilderness areas,' forgetting that all the world is hers."[50] The worst sin of all, for Berry, is wilderness as tourist escape—elevating the wilderness to an impossible paradise, seeking in it some temporary transcendence, and then returning to domestic places where all things wild are considered dangerous.

The essay arrives in epigrammatic sections, almost a sequence of prose poems. His style here—and his message—closely mirror that of Williams. Both writers know the wilderness unsettles us because it came before us and will likely outlast us. "Wilderness is the source of what we can imagine and what we cannot," Williams says.[51]

Wilderness is "the tap root of consciousness. It will survive us."[52] Williams is one of the most lyric defenders of the natural world—particularly in the American West. The language and mode of her defense capture what she calls the "glorious indifference" of the wilderness both in content and in form. Her narratives are often written in short paragraphs and metaphorical thoughts, like journals. In this way, they reveal the personal nature of the wilderness while simultaneously remaining incomplete as narratives—thus demonstrating her theme that the wilderness exists beyond and without us.

Although she was born in California in 1955, Williams grew up in Salt Lake City, Utah. The lake and its environs are setting and metaphor in her work. As a child, she hiked and birdwatched in the nearby Bear River Migratory Bird Sanctuary. She studied English and biology at the state university and later received a graduate degree in environmental education. Shortly afterward, she began working at the Museum of Natural History and served as naturalist-in-residence for a decade. Her early publications were nature-focused children's books as well as nonfiction for adults—work centered in her own version of Mormon spirituality and storytelling.[53]

Although Williams's Utah setting is different from Berry's Kentucky, their lives and lineages are wedded to the land. "I've never really been able to separate family, spirituality, landscape, and home," Williams explains.[54] For four generations, her family "has made a living by putting in natural gas lines, water lines, sewage lines, optic fiber cables. Our family has made its livelihood from the land, digging trenches for hundreds of miles cross-country."[55] She is aware of the tension of love and destruction of the land, but like Berry, Williams is an environmental realist—if we are to unite the wild and the domestic, the wilderness with the human, then we must accept their inherent conflicts. The key, for Williams, is how we treat the wilderness: "respecting the land, the wildlife, the plants, the rivers, mountains, and deserts, the absolute essential bedrock of our lives."[56]

Another complex bedrock of Williams's life is her Mormon identity. She married her husband, Brooke, in a Mormon temple in Salt Lake City in 1975, when she was nineteen. "I was raised to believe in a spirit world," Williams says, and "if the natural world was assigned spiritual values, then those days spent in wildness were sacred. We learned at an early age that God can be found wherever you are, especially outside."[57]

Utah land—a place of "isolation and a landscape of grit"—was "just what the Mormons were looking for. A land that no one else wanted meant religious freedom and community-building without persecution."[58] The particular wilderness of the Great Basin Desert "was familiar to them if not by sight, at least by story."[59] Those religious stories formed Williams's vision of the wild. She recalls sitting in church as a child and listening to the stories of Christ's struggle in the wilderness and how that place is where he reclaimed his strength. As an adult, she affirms this complex identity: "I am a Mormon woman. I am not orthodox. It is the lens through which I see the world. I hear the Tabernacle Choir and it still makes me weep. There are other things within the culture that absolutely enrage me, and for me it is sacred rage."[60]

Much of her sacred rage is focused on the Great Salt Lake, that "wilderness adjacent to a city."[61] She describes the lake as "a shifting shoreline that plays havoc with highways; islands too stark, too remote to inhabit; water in the desert that no one can drink."[62] It is a trickster lake, the "liquid lie of the West."[63] In the "forsaken corners" of the lake, "there is no illusion of being safe. You stand in the throbbing silence of the Great Basin, exposed and alone."[64]

Despite that silence and lack of comfort, Williams notes it is "strange how deserts turn us into believers."[65] Her writing is sustained by that belief. Williams writes united in sound and spirit with her landscape. Her descriptions of place are gorgeous: "Dusk is approaching. Meadowlarks and yellow-headed blackbirds sing the shadows longer. Lake Bonneville has left its mark. Bathtub rings rim the Great Basin. Tonight these mountains are lavender with blue creases that fall like chintz."[66]

Despite this beauty, her work is suffused with a melancholy sense. She laments the state of the wilderness in the West and the continual need for activism. In *Refuge*, her sadness is personal: Williams's mother is dying of cancer. A mother's womb, she writes, "is the first landscape we inhabit. It is here we learn to respond—to move, to listen, to be nourished and grow."[67] The metaphor evolves when her mother dies. Then Williams returns to the lake, where she once again feels "free" but is spiritually changed: "Dogma doesn't hold me. Wildness does."[68] She describes the premise of her storytelling as the idea "that an intimacy with the natural world initiates an intimacy with death, because life and death are engaged in an endless, inseparable dance."[69] Williams believes that intimacy comes from our conceptions of home. Like Berry, she worries that if we place wilderness at a distance—even with the best intentions of preservation—then we risk erasing our natural intimacy with the wild.

She illustrates this with an anecdote from her time at the American Museum of Natural History in New York. She worked with someone whose sense of place "was rooted in Pelham Bay Park, near the Bronx."[70] They went on a collecting trip for invertebrates, and Williams was first "horrified at what the people in New York considered 'wetlands.'"[71] But then she "realized that it takes so little to sustain life that, even in these wetlands that had been drained, dredged, and dumped in, there was life in all its vitality—even a Black Crowned Night heron standing in the reeds staring at us."[72] Williams needed to realize that for her coworker, Pelham Bay was her home, her personal landscape, "a sanctuary she holds inside her unguarded heart."[73] The birds' songs are what kept her "attentive in a city that has little memory of wildness."[74]

Those patches of wildness in New York City not only gave Williams hope but also reaffirmed her belief that wilderness "is not a belief. It is a place"—a place among us.[75] Her place begins with the Great Salt Lake but extends to Utah as a whole and the area of the Colorado Plateau. There, one "cannot help but be undone by its sensibility and light, nothing extra. Before the stillness of sandstone cliffs, you stand still, equally bare."[76]

This is Williams's essential wilderness: the red rock canyons of southern Utah. "Short on green,"[77] they are not the forests of Berry. "Green recalls pastoral comfort, provides a resting place for the eyes."[78] The desert is without escape—a place steeped in the "harsh, brutal beauty of skin and bones."[79] This desert is not a vast, flat expanse but a desert of descent, with canyons, rivers, and "washes left dry, scoured, and sculpted by sporadic flash floods."[80] Such geography colors a writer's vision, and Williams feels like her character has been shaped by the "rugged truth of indifference" that comes from "mountain ranges and arid basins, sagebrush oceans, grasslands, high deserts and plateaus, wild and raging rivers."[81] Her conclusion: "Wilderness is a place of humility. Humility is a place of wilderness."[82] This glorious wilderness is indifferent to even those who capture its beauty. Williams accepts this indifference not as callous; one fallacy of demanding a personal communion with nature is expecting that communion to occur on terms other than our mere appreciation of that wilderness. Williams seeks to affirm the importance of wilderness through our awe—the recognition that the wild is more than us.

Humility allows us to become one with the wilderness again, and that union can be transformative. Williams recalls visiting the Prado Museum in Madrid, where she became obsessed with *The Garden of Earthly Delights*, an expansive and macabre triptych by Hieronymus Bosch. She brings her binoculars to the museum and makes a checklist of all the birds she sees in the painting. "My mind becomes wild in the presence of creation, the artist's creation," she writes.[83] Enraptured with Bosch, Williams wonders why we don't "designate wilderness as an installation of art? Conceptual art?"[84] Lost in Bosch's meandering, frolicking characters, and his absurdities, Williams concludes that "we can never be tamed completely."[85] Our natural state is to be wild.

Bosch's wild world is not the American West that Williams loves, but those worlds share a disorienting sense: a surreal feeling of otherness. The wilderness does this to us. When Williams says that it is "hard to take yourself very seriously when confronted face-to-face with a mountain lion or the reality of no water in the desert," she is implying that nature forces our sense of humility—but she could just as easily have used those examples to describe how the bare wilderness shocks and startles us alive.[86] This is also how the wilderness does the work of the spirit. Williams says she courts rather than fears the heart of the wild. She longs to "touch stone, rock, water, the trunks of trees, the sway of grasses, the barbs of a feather, the fur left behind by a shedding bison"—this is what helps her find a sense of belief.[87]

"I return to the wilderness," she explains, "to remember what I have forgotten, that the world can be wholesome and beautiful, that the harmony and integrity of ecosystems at peace is a mirror to what we have lost."[88] In order to experience this mirror, we must walk a careful path: attempt to conserve and preserve the wild around us but not mistake this curation for control. Williams offers our national parks system as an example. "No matter how much we try to manage and manipulate, orchestrate, or regulate" those parks, "they will remain as the edge-scapes they are, existing on the boundaries between culture and wildness—improvisational spaces immune to the scripts of anyone."[89] Wildlife surprises us. We get joyfully lost: "For a precious moment we touch and taste life uninterrupted. Awe sneaks up on us like love. We surrender to the ecstatic outpouring of life before us."[90]

It is not surprising that Williams, open to the ecstasy and strangeness of the wilderness, would laud a defense of it by a sensuous writer such as D. H. Lawrence. In his preface to *Lady Chatterley's Lover*, his controversial novel, Lawrence writes of the taboo of wilderness: "Oh, what a catastrophe for man when he cut himself off from the rhythm of the year, from his unison with the sun and the earth."[91] Williams makes that connection again through her activism but most acutely through her acts of creation.

"I have felt the pain that arises from a recognition of beauty, pain we hold when we remember what we are connected to and the delicacy of our relations," Williams writes—speaking of the love for her late mother as well as the tenuous wilderness around her.[92] Her writing is born from these tender connections so that writing "becomes an act of compassion toward life, the life we so often refuse to see because if we look too closely or feel too deeply, there may be no end to our suffering. But words empower us, move us beyond our suffering, and set us free. This is the sorcery of literature. We are healed by our stories."[93]

We are healed, then, by wilderness—despite its indifference to us. Our healing occurs in the wild because there, we are most acutely aware of our bodies and their limitations. Our senses are heightened, and we perceive the divine in nature. We must accept the paradoxes of those spaces. The wilderness is gentle and dangerous; it resists our good-natured attempts to support it. The wilderness grows and grows, and it flows—on its own terms. Berry reminds us that we "began in a world that was pristine, undiminished by anything we had done, and at various times in our history the unspoiled wilderness has again imposed itself, its charming and forbidding *invitation*, upon our consciousness."[94] We have to learn to love the wilderness again in its natural, truest sense. We "need the experience of leaving something alone."[95] Only then might the wilderness serve "as a standard of civilization and as a cultural model. Only by preserving areas where nature's processes are undisturbed can we preserve an accurate sense of the impact of civilization upon its natural sources."[96]

Yet Berry cautions that "we cannot hope—for reasons practical and humane, we cannot even wish—to preserve more than a small portion of the land in wilderness. Most of it we will have to use."[97] He shares this sentiment with Williams. If we consider the border between wild and domestic to be a porous one, then it follows that wilderness must be encountered at some point. Berry reminds us, though, that we are foolish to think that this implies our *control* of wilderness; rather, we are merely participating in an old story.

We have to go back to those old ways. For Berry and Williams, we have to return our senses to the time before they were dulled by the perspective of industry, when "we began to romanticize the wilderness—which is to say we began to institutionalize it within the concept of the 'scenic.'"[98] Railroads and highways offered an escape from the arduous wilderness. The wilderness was no longer a place to be climbed or forded but instead "something to be looked at as grand or beautiful from the high vantages of the roadside."[99] We traded a sense of beauty for reality—the reality that "wilderness still circumscribed civilization and persisted in domesticity."[100] The result has been a dangerous one: "We forgot, indeed, that the civilized and the domestic continued to *depend* upon wilderness—that is, upon natural forces within the climate and within the soil that have never in any meaningful sense been controlled or conquered."[101]

In order to remember, we must go back. We often don't need to travel far. Wildness surrounds us—and it requires not a new way of looking at the world but an old, ancient method. When asked what gives her hope, Williams answers, "Two words: forgiveness and restoration."[102] Both can be gained by going back to the wild places that we have forsaken. We must be ready to face the glorious indifference of the wilderness; in fact, we must embrace it.

4

Ghosts Demand More

Jim Harrison and Thomas McGuane

Speaking of a friendship that spanned half a century, Thomas McGuane said he and Jim Harrison bolstered each other with "a fairly high view of the mission of writing, so that in lean years and blocked times it still felt that it was kind of a religious commitment."[1] It is difficult to find two contemporary fiction writers who were more important to each other—and whose bond is forged deeper in the spirit of the wilderness—than Harrison and McGuane. They imagine the wilderness as a place of ritual and rejuvenation, where we may connect to an ancient and mysterious tradition. The wilderness is a place of tension and conflict—where savagery can occur—but it is also a reserve for creativity. Although McGuane and Harrison could be sarcastic and jaundiced about humans, they were mystical and earnest about the wild: they acknowledged that the wilderness should demand our respect.

Both writers are from Michigan—born three hours away from each other (Harrison in Grayling, on the Upper Peninsula, and McGuane in Wyandotte, near Lake Erie)—but did not meet until they were undergraduates at Michigan State. They both grew old out west. McGuane moved to Montana in 1968, and Harrison joined him in Big Sky Country in 2002. He also lived in Patagonia, Arizona, where he died, pen in hand, writing a poem.

A passing appropriate for a legend—yet Harrison never did much to cultivate his own mythos. He taught at a college for a few years but found more independence outside the academy. He was never a recluse. He was a traveler, but he wasn't hiding from anything. He said that he never got ideas while sitting still. "Someone has to stay outside," he believed.[2] Harrison was called toward the wilderness.

That call began in his childhood. When he was three, his family moved from Grayling to Reed City, a bit south on the Upper Peninsula. The family had spent some time living with Harrison's maternal grandparents, and he long remembered waking "to the animal sounds that seem to comfort one, easing the soul into consciousness" on their farm.[3] When he was seven, Harrison got in an argument with a girl who "shoved a broken bottle in my face and my sight had leaked away with a lot of blood."[4]

He lost vision in the eye and fled to the woods: "I'd turn for solace to rivers, rain, trees, birds, lakes, animals. If things are terrible beyond conception and I walk for twenty-five miles in the forest, they tend to go away for a while."[5] It became a lifelong mark and metaphor. "My left eye is blind and jogs like / a milky sparrow in its socket," he writes in an early poem, stressing that his sense of perception and being will always remain blurred.[6] The traumatic event was memorialized in spiritual terms: "Now self is the first sacrament / who loves not the misery and taint / of the present tense is lost."[7] Jarred from lost sense and sight, Harrison felt lodged in the melancholy of his past.

As a "consolation" for his injury, his father and brothers built "a cabin on a remote lake fifteen miles from town" with "huge gulleys covered by bracken and the large stumps of white pines cut in the logging era, small bogs and lakes, some too shallow for fish, grand swamps, and ridges covered with birch, oak, maple, and beech."[8] The Upper Peninsula of his youth "was wild, crisscrossed by old logging roads" and the perfect place for a boy to get lost: "The natural world can draw away your poisons to the point that your curiosity takes over and 'you,' the accumulation of wounds and concomitant despair, no longer exist."[9]

Harrison preferred the Portuguese concept of *saudade* to describe how the wilderness shaped his soul over the course of his life. Saudade, for Harrison, is marked by someone, some place, or some sense of life "irretrievably lost; a shadow of your own making that follows you."[10] When this shadow emerges from the darkness, it creates "heartache, an obtuse sentimentality, a sharp anger that you are not located where you wish to be."[11] However "an irrational and childish melancholy" this feeling might be, it was powerful and created a sense of abject longing for Harrison.[12] The wilderness was the locus of these feelings, a place where he lost sight yet could never stop looking. The woods—wide, wild, and surreal—became a place of ritual for him.

His parents, though, wanted Harrison and his siblings to be closer to Michigan State, where they might later attend, so the family moved to Haslett when he was twelve. Harrison wasn't happy: "I was going to a place where there weren't any rivers, no trout, no cabin (which was being sold to my uncles), no loons or blue herons, no bobcats, no endless forests to wander in."[13] The distance—as distance does—made his childhood woods even more mythic. The legend of his wilderness became permanent.

With his physical wilderness gone, Harrison experienced a "religious upheaval."[14] He was "saved" at a Baptist revival at fourteen.[15] He wanted a feeling of ecstasy and soon had strange and uncomfortable visions: "the hem of Isaiah's robe stretching miles across a seascape, all the different creatures in the world drinking milk from an immense golden bowl, the perilous caves, and passageways inhabited by evil spirits that changed shapes."[16] He read the New Testament again and again but "found it quite devoid of my minister's attitudes toward culture."[17] Harrison's religious sense was ecstatic, surreal, encompassing—but his elders were staid and traditional. His teenage fervor calmed.

His acute religious years, which included a brief stint as a preacher, had "adapted themselves to art as a religion."[18] Yet that cryptic statement is often misread. Harrison was never an unbeliever, and he was certainly not a practicing Buddhist, as he is sometimes rendered. Here was a young man who had visions of Isaiah, a desert prophet—not at all surprising, considering his hypnotic pull toward the wilderness.

Harrison couldn't survive as a textbook preacher; instead, he is better understood as a Christian mystic. "I suppose I am essentially Christian because that is my mythos," he has said.[19] His Christian mythos was revealed through ritual. As an adult, he would pray in the morning and then read and write poetry. The process was "mythical in origin and the energy behind the mythological transfers from one form to another. And you think San Juan de la Cruz or Santa Teresa, these improbably fabulous poets, who were also very devout poets, but for some reason this is now totally unacceptable."[20] His Christianity, like other moments of those defining years, "becomes embedded in your spirit."[21] He never wavered in that belief: "I realized a couple of years ago that never has it occurred to me not to believe in God and Jesus, and all that."[22]

Another change was happening for Harrison: he felt drawn to literature. He said it "was a difficult thing to discover Jesus and Keats and James Joyce all at the same time. Your soul is pulling all these other directions."[23] "Only much later in my life," Harrison concluded, "did I come to understand that there was a bridge between my early life in the natural world and the arena of literature, music, and painting."[24]

Young Harrison played football for Haslett High School, read, hunted, and fished. He lied about his age to work as a busboy at a hotel in Colorado and engaged in some misadventures. His father, aware of his literary interests, got him a typewriter for his seventeenth birthday. Taken with the literary life, he went with a friend to Greenwich Village in New York City during the summer and brought books by Rimbaud, Faulkner, Dostoyevsky, and Joyce and the King James Bible.

He fell in love with poetry back home, among nature. He sat on the roof of his house in Michigan and watched "the moon rise over a big marsh" where "birds of various species were crisscrossing the moon and I could see them clearly in silhouette."[25] Around that time, the popular poet and critic John Ciardi, fresh off his iconic translation of *The Inferno*, became the poetry editor of *Saturday Review*. He announced his editorial mission in an article titled "Everyone Writes (Bad) Poetry," beginning with a lament: "The office mailbag bulges daily with envelopes full of bad poems that bear paper-clipped to them laborious little notes that breathe, however shyly, the most grandiose hopes."[26] One such note was sent by Harrison. The ambitious young Harrison sent Ciardi a poem titled "The Existentialist," which he said, was influenced by Jean-Paul Sartre and Søren Kierkegaard. Ciardi didn't publish the poem. Undeterred, Harrison kept writing—earning undergraduate and graduate degrees at nearby Michigan State—and within a decade, the poet and editor Denise Levertov released *Plain Song*, Harrison's debut, with W. W. Norton.

Poetry suited his wild heart. "I have an inordinate amount of time to think and wander around," he said.[27] His knack for writing and selling screenplays was a lucrative pursuit; unconcerned with making money off his fiction and poetry and unmoored by the culture of academia, he could create freely. Poetry was his fount, his refrain. He published nearly a thousand poems across fourteen books.

The poems in *Plain Song* unfold as pastoral pieces set in northern Michigan. Here are back roads where "stump fences surround nothing / worth their tearing down // by a deserted filling station / a Veedol sign, the rusted hulk // of a Frazer, 'live bait' / on battered tin."[28] He writes of the county fair, where a "buck- / toothed girl cuts her honorable-mention / cake; when she leans to get me water / from a milk pail her breasts are chaste."[29] Later at the fair, sitting in his car, he "think[s] of St. Paul's Epistles and pray[s] / the removal of what my troubled eyes have seen."[30]

"Form is the woods," he writes in another poem—an apt way to understand his poetic structure and visceral setting.[31] In the poem, a bobcat stalks a pheasant in the wilderness, which silently encompasses the drama: "trees, rich green, the moving of boughs / and the separate leaf, yield / to conclusions they do not care about / or watch—the dead, frayed bird."[32] The bobcat kills the bird, but the forest goes on: the wilderness will outlast all of us.

Harrison's sense of the wilderness is sustained by two complex, recurring metaphors in his writing: thickets and rivers. These metaphors appear in his poems, interviews, essays, and stories. They are a bridge between the physical and spiritual world, between his childhood and maturity. His obsession with thickets began after his childhood eye injury, when he fled to the woods and felt safest in enclosed spaces—thorned and thatched, branches intertwined into a roof and room to shield him from the world. "I'm still informed by the same thickets I was looking for at age seven," Harrison said, and thickets even crept back into his dreams.[33] He jokingly referred to them as his "solace thickets," but the description is accurate.[34]

For Harrison, a great thicket affords seclusion but does not hide the world. You must be able to enter the thicket and see out, but no one can notice you within the growth. Harrison has never wanted the world to disappear, but rather, he wanted to observe it in silence. Thickets "offer me peace in a life that is permanently inconsolable but reasonably vital and productive. Thickets quickly draw off the poison. After a few minutes of sitting you hear your own tentative heartbeat."[35] He considers these thickets to be "my functioning churches" where "I tend not to pray" but "let my mind alone until it empties out."[36]

Harrison's characters also find spiritual peace in thickets. His story "The Woman Lit by Fireflies" begins with Clare and Donald, who are driving home from visiting their daughter and are now on the way to visit their son. The visit with their daughter was cut short because Donald had gotten in an argument with her. No one is surprised; Donald has always been acerbic.

Exhausted from a headache, Clare pulls over at a rest stop, goes into the bathroom, and writes a note for the police that her husband has been abusing her. She sneaks out of the building and climbs a fence, and then "she hurried off down between two corn rows, toward the interior, wherever that might be."[37] Her head continues to hurt, so she dizzily drifts further into the cornfield. The deeper she moves from asphalt and machines, the more mystical Harrison's writing becomes: "By the time the sun made its way down through the tassels, leaves and stalks, it was weak and liquid. There was a crow call so close it startled her, the bird flapping low over her row, then twisting, darting back for another look, squawking loudly in warning at the intruder, then a third pass up the row out of curiosity. She had never been so close to a crow, she thought."[38]

No longer suffocated by her husband, Clare can now drift, alone, in the wild of the rows. She loses a sense of time and finds herself in a "dense thicket, apparently as impenetrable as any of the topiary hedges she had seen in England and France. The thicket grew into the cornfield so she couldn't turn right or left."[39] A burgeoning thunderstorm sends her into the "makeshift cave" of the thicket, and she thinks about her life.[40]

Tired and isolated in this partial wilderness, Clare enters a spiritual state, coaxed by the "half-dozen fireflies" that "gathered in the darkness around her green cave, and the tiny beams seemed to trace the convolutions of her thought."[41] Much like Harrison himself, Clare undergoes a transformation in this thicket; she "was sinking into the ground," her "body sweet, warm, deadened, giving itself up to the bed of leaves and grass, the green odor transmitting a sense she belonged to the earth as much as any other living thing."[42]

The fireflies remain above her, "blinking off and on, whirling toward each other so if you blurred your eyes there were tracers, yellow lines of light everywhere."[43] Lit by their bodies, Clare suddenly "felt blessed without thinking whether or not she deserved it. She went back to her nest, lay down and wept for a few minutes, then watched a firefly hovering barely a foot above her head."[44]

Harrison and his characters find true comfort in these fortified spaces, but they also are drawn to bodies of water. In fact, Harrison has said, "I've come to think of rivers as moving thickets, truly lovely and safe places."[45] Like thickets, rivers are places of spiritual rejuvenation: "If you're willing to give up everything, or open up a bit, the river does absorb rather nonchalantly your poisons and after a while there's just nothing there but you and the river and you're not confusing your separateness at all. The river is the river. But it's really done a marvelous bit on you."[46]

The first lines of his memoir *Off to the Side* unfold by water. He writes of going on walks shortly after dawn, no matter where he is staying. He will go anywhere in nature—"empty fields, canyons, woods"—but he prefers to be "near a creek or river because since childhood I've loved the sound they make. Moving water is forever in the present tense, a condition we rather achingly avoid."[47] He also loves the water at night, recalling that "strange fragrance to a river at night that I've never been able to identify, some water-washed mixture of fern, rotting poplar, cedar, and the earthen odor of logjams."[48]

Rivers run into Harrison's poems. In "The Theory and Practice of Rivers," he writes of the "rivers of my life," including how the shape of water flow is reflected in so many other elements of life and images: "roots of plants and trees, / certain coral heads, / photos of splintered lightning, / blood vessels, / the shapes of creeks and rivers."[49] The wilderness is embedded in our anatomy, our atmosphere, and where we live—its symbols a wellspring of communion. Later in the poem, the narrator goes out into the natural world while grieving: "After a month of interior weeping / it occurred to me that in times like these / I have nothing to fall back on / except the sun and moon and earth."[50] The wilderness accepts our grief, for its wildness has suffered and survived. Fallen trees cross a forest like a graveyard, and growth overtakes the dead—offering a metaphor for our own pain and spiritual need.

That melancholy sense returns gracefully in other poems. His rivers are "moving looms of light."[51] Rivers become elegiac, the stuff of life's end: "The days, at last, are stacked against / what we think we are. / Who in their most hallowed, sleepless / night with the moon seven feet / outside the window, the moon / that the river swallows, would wish / it otherwise?"[52]

Rivers are the itinerant wilderness: the unstoppable, beautiful routes that transcend town and region and even perhaps time. To borrow a word from the fiction writer John Gardner, rivers are *profluent*—forward moving and present—in the same way that great writing is profluent. One of Harrison's most profluent and river-steeped books is *A Good Day to Die*, his provocative second novel. Despite being a profoundly pessimistic book about drugs and discontent in the shadow of the Vietnam War, the story's environmental message resonates, offering the sclerotic characters some hope.

Early in the novel, the narrator, fishing in Key West, Florida, is at a bar when he notices a long-haired, muscular man glaring at him from across the bar. He sees an eagle tattoo on the man's forearm and how a "bleached twist of scar tissue" turned the man's eyes "a few degrees off center."[53] The narrator has never met Tim, the tattooed Vietnam veteran, but in the spirit of the novel's misanthropy, they embark on a cross-country journey. The pair decides to go west to blow up dams that have been built to stop the natural flow of rivers, the type of waterways they love to fish. "I was along for the ride," the narrator says as they stop to pick up Tim's girlfriend, Sylvia. "Maybe we would do something interesting. If we blew up some dam it would have a sort of final interest to it like a fishing record that couldn't be taken away from you."[54]

Their harebrained plan has a whisper of altruism: they seek to reclaim the wilderness from those who would stop it. Yet the plan is better than the reality. The narrator describes his feeling once they arrive in Wyoming, closer to their destination: "Now in the first light, standing in the gravel parking lot, all of my berserk enthusiasm, fed by Tim's speed talk and my imagination and a dozen tapes in the deck, had vanished. The landscape was bleak and the air already warm."[55] Now much closer to the actual wilderness—and not merely the wilderness of their mythos—they lose their bravado. The narrator would rather simply experience the crisp nature of the West. While the others sleep, he walks out of the cabin, and sitting "in the cool dark I felt more conscious than I had in the previous eight days and I rather liked this unexpected awareness."[56]

The purity and beauty of the rivers they sought to protect now become more important than the violent action of that protection. The narrator is instead transfixed, feeling that there is "a strangeness to the morning that disturbed me and at first I attributed it to the similarity of walking to the river as I had walked to so many rivers on so many dawns."[57] Once that reverie passes, the narrator returns to what brought him out west in the first place: that his action would be considered a protest to help save a small section of wilderness. He considers that "fishing friends would admire me for doing what many fishermen thought of frequently."[58]

Not all goes well. The group blows up a dam in Orofino, Idaho, but Tim is killed in the blast. Their dream of wilderness protection is revealed to be merely a crime—a short-sighted attempt to save water that becomes an act of destruction. This is a dark ending for the novel but not an altogether surprising one. Despite Harrison's belief that the wilderness can offer spiritual healing, he also ascribes a certain melancholy and morbidity to the wild. Even though we might sometimes become one with the wilderness, it remains beyond us.

Harrison has said the natural world, including in his fiction, is "not very romantic. . . . It's not always very pleasant in our human terms."[59] This is more acute than the indifference of Wendell Berry and Terry Tempest Williams. Harrison's wilderness exists without regard for human constructs of morality. It is not evil; it is other. Such fierceness is present in his story "Revenge," in which Harrison's language of nature is provocative. The novella's first sentence—"You could not tell if you were a bird descending (and there was a bird descending, a vulture) if the naked man was dead or alive"—arrives in almost convoluted syntax, replicating what could be rigor mortis.[60] The crooked descent of the bird in that first sentence is justified because the "man didn't know himself" if he was dead or alive. After all, "carrion was shared not by the shearer's design but by a pattern set before anyone knew there were patterns."[61]

The man's expiration is watched not only by the vulture but also by a coyote, her pups, and an old male coyote whose "belly was full of javelina and watching this dying man was simply the most interesting thing to happen his way in a long time."[62] There's no hymn to nature here: "It was all curiosity though: when the man died the coyote would simply walk away and leave it to the vultures."[63] The coyote had been watching even "when the naked man had been thrown from the car the night before."[64] And with that tease, Harrison ends the first section of the tale. But the man is not dead yet. Harrison pulls us forward with the man in a coma, his identity of much interest to certain Mexican locals. With the calm yet pointed narration he employs elsewhere, Harrison slowly reveals the identity of this man, Cochran, who "saw his beating as a long thread that led back from his immediate present, from this room almost to his birth."[65] Even in a story saturated with violence, Harrison implies a mystical sense to the natural world—an order greater than us that we are not meant to understand.

The natural wild might be dangerous, but it might also be beautiful; regardless, it is always slightly beyond us. The wilderness for Harrison is always an otherworldly place. He recalls how a magazine once asked him to write about nature, but "I told them I couldn't write about nature but I'd write them a little piece about getting lost and all the profoundly good aspects of being lost—the immense fresh feeling of really being lost."[66] Being lost is the "ultimate level of attentiveness," the most profound way of being and creating.[67] Harrison could be lost in nature because he offers himself to it. In fact, he wonders why others are unable to do the same: "Why are people incapable of ascribing to the natural world the kind of mystery which they think they are somehow deserving of but have never reached?"[68]

Attention to the mysteries of the wilderness can afford creative results. Harrison often got his ideas from going for walks in the woods and from his dreams—since both experiences enabled him to capture a latent mystical sense. His introduction to *Just before Dark*, his collected nonfiction, captures this feeling: "Walking at twilight owns the same eeriness of dawn. The world belongs again to its former prime tenants, the creatures, and within the dimming light and crisp shadows, you return to your own creature life that is so easily and ordinarily discarded. I have always loved best this time just before dark when the antennae stretch far and caressingly from the body."[69] Harrison felt that dreams "emerged" from the landscape itself, another spiritual connection between humans and the wild.[70]

If we are connected to the wilderness, then we must treat it with care. Harrison admitted his own youthful sins of illegal fishing and hunting, when he fancied himself "a steely half-breed Robert Mitchum type with hatchet, revolver, cartridge belt and a long mane of hair trained with bear grease."[71] Young Harrison accepted what Edward Abbey called a bastardization of the cowboy mythos, that the wilderness is "endless, unspoiled, mysterious, still remaining to be overcome and finally won."[72]

Harrison recognized that we can't love the wilderness if we treat it as land to be conquered; we will never find spiritual peace in those places if their existence is contingent on our whims. "It's not wilderness anyway," Harrison clarified, "if it only exists by our permission and stewardship."[73] He was interested not in owning or controlling the wilderness but in communing with it. "An enemy of civilization," Harrison writes in "Drinking Song," "I want to walk around in the woods, fish and drink. / I'm going to be a child about it and I can't help it."[74] Art springs from the wilderness. Harrison thought language is most vivid when it is tied to the natural world: "plants, animals both farm and wild, trees, weather, land and water shapes, the sun, moon, and stars."[75]

The material of nature compelled a calm melancholy in Harrison's poetry and prose. Many writers settle into melancholy and sentiment in their later works—when death is on the horizon—but Harrison had a mystical vision from his early writing. In a poem from *Returning to Earth*, he writes, at "nineteen I began to degenerate, / slight smell of death in my gestures."[76] And he feels resigned to his end: "Let the scavenger take what he finds. / Let the predator love his prey."[77] The poems of the final decades of his life tended to be characterized by a few recurring traits or themes: visceral description of the outdoors, a playful tone by turns mystical and surreal, and the consistent presence of his broken body. In those ways, a mystical sense of the wild is incongruous with the trite and maudlin. "Sentimentality forgets what it is to be wild," Harrison warns—imploring poets to get out into nature and experience it.[78] Nature-starved poets who write about the wild create "a kind of breathless nature poem from people totally uninformed about the natural world in terms of botany or ornithology. But it's a set piece, like in Victorian England there were all these faux sincere set pieces."[79]

That's the type of sarcastic comment that Harrison might make to McGuane, either in person or on paper. Their shared affinity for the often unforgiving wilderness made them oddities in the literary world but perfect for each other. They became close at Michigan State and only increased their personal and professional bond.

Harrison was instrumental in getting McGuane's debut novel, *The Sporting Club*, published at Simon & Schuster. The novel is exactly the type of darkly comic farce that Harrison would appreciate. In the book's first scene, old friends reunite at a Michigan hunting and fishing club and promptly engage in a basement duel. One fells the other with a pair of wax bullets. It's easy to imagine this as Harrison and McGuane themselves, one bruised from the fake rounds, the other twirling his pistol, both cackling together in the Michigan wilderness.

McGuane's family had moved from Massachusetts to Michigan before he was born. They felt out of place: "We saw ourselves as Catholics surrounded by Protestant mid-westerners."[80] McGuane attended Catholic school but clarified his particular strand of faith: "There are two kinds of Irish Catholicism: one is the real intense, regular mass attendance kind; the other is where it's a received part of your culture. You're more culturally a Catholic, very often, than you are religiously a Catholic."[81] McGuane admitted "an inchoate pining for religion" in which he saw "spirituality in the processes of natural renewal, in creation as it were."[82] "I am very comfortable considering myself an Irish-Catholic," he concludes, "implying, as it does to me, a superimposition of the life of Christ upon earth-worshipping pantheism. Like Flannery O'Connor, I frequently portray people in purgatory, hence the irreligious atmosphere."[83]

He describes his mother's side of the family as "heavy-duty Irish," "fantastic storytellers" who "really valued wise-cracks and uncanny stories—that was the structure of life in that house, and the really unforgivable sin was to go on too long."[84] Yet McGuane was skeptical about the "influence of storytelling on my writing. I don't think of myself particularly as a storyteller. My passion is language and human perception, not necessarily in the form of stories."[85]

McGuane is one of the most talented stylists at the sentence level; he appears utterly in control of his syntax and sound. His talent was on display from his first novel, the book Harrison helped him publish: *The Sporting Club*. McGuane has talked about using "satire as a purgative," a way to pare back the absurdities of language and society to reach a purer, more natural wildness.[86] The novel begins with James Quinn returning to the Centennial Club, a sporting club in the Michigan woods, founded by logger barons in 1868. He is going to be reunited with the unpredictable Vernor Stanton, a childhood friend.

Steeped in practical jokes, the novel is a sarcastic whirlwind of tomfoolery—clearly the work of a young writer having fun. But McGuane's sentimental view of nature breaks through the flippancy. Late in the novel, Quinn goes night fishing to escape Stanton's constant bravado. He heads for the river, "not undertaking this fishing lightly. The night was warm and creaky, the round spring moon figured with bats and moths."[87] Here he truly feels home; he thinks about "how the long hours of staring at the mutable silky river often left him dazed for a day after."[88]

Only the wilderness could save Quinn: "The darkness encouraged his dreaming and replaced Stanton's lunacies with heavy trout that threshed the smooth and moon-yellowed river."[89] The reverie is broken by an explosion back at the club, but the effect is clear: from his earliest book, McGuane had a predilection toward the wilderness as a place of rejuvenation. And fishing, above all other encounters with nature, was the most kenotic.

Fishing is a "respite from burden" for McGuane, and that gentle escape started in his youth.[90] "Early on," he explains, "I decided that fishing would be my way of looking at the world. First it taught me how to look at rivers. Lately it has been teaching me how to look at people, myself included."[91] His invocations—on this subject only—are downright religious: "The Bible tells us to watch and listen. Something like this suggests what fishing ought to be about: using the ceremony of our sport and passion to arouse greater reverberations within ourselves."[92]

As a boy, he fished on Lake Erie for perch, rock bass, and pike. After his time at Michigan State, his Stegner fellowship, and a graduate degree from the Yale School of Drama, McGuane's fishing life split between Key West and Montana, where he has lived since 1968. His writing about fishing there is among his most lyric and layered, devoid of satire but still steeped in the technical skill that has defined his fiction.

Fishing creates McGuane's communion with the wilderness. He writes of a "possession" that occurs during angling—when you "watch the river flowing, the insects landing and hatching, the places where trout hold, and to insinuate the supple, binding movement of tapered line until, when the combination is right, the line becomes rigid and many of its motions are conceived at the other end."[93] The water is downright baptismal; "Only in the observation of nature," McGuane writes, "can we recover that view of eternity that consoled our forebears."[94] In words that evoke Harrison, McGuane says that "moving water has, all my life, been the most constant passion I've had."[95]

In the tradition of other great writers of wilderness, McGuane is able to evoke transcendence through finite experiences. His description of the flora and water of Montana are among his most beautiful writing. There, in spring, a warm wind arrives "before anything turns green, though not quite before some birds—owls and juncos for example—nest and even begin to hatch their young."[96] The "brightest thing in the landscape" is the sagebrush buttercup, which has arrived so early "that it follows the retreating snow in a yellow haze."[97]

In those moments, a creek seems "pellucid, throwing the shadows of trout on its graveled bottom, and on others milky with low country runoff."[98] He then slows time to focus on a trout "held in a bar of current, his pink stripe shone up through the cold green water of springtime."[99] He contemplates that moment—how precise experiences in the wilderness can almost become ethereal visions—before letting the trout back into the water.

These flowing, free spaces are McGuane's true wilderness. "An undisturbed river," he writes, "is as perfect a thing as we will ever know, every refractive slide of cold water a glimpse of eternity."[100] He finds happiness there: a sense of glee so radical that "I sometimes wondered if there wasn't something misanthropic in this passion for solitude."[101]

There might be. McGuane's early sarcasm and style have evolved into more of a smirk than a scowl. Even his later fiction about the wild feels different. "Stars," one of his many stories to appear in the *New Yorker*, begins with a character named Jessica walking along Cascade Creek, "a sparkling crevice in a vast bed of spruce needles," where "light descended the trunks and ignited balsamic forest odors, awakening the birds and making it easy to find stepping stones to cross the narrow creek."[102] She follows the creek to where the water "fell through a tangle of evergreen roots to form a plunge pool."[103] She sits and watches "the movement of bubbles into its crystalline depths, lost in her thoughts, free of history. Time was not the same dimension here that it was in the rest of her life, and floating like this was something to be savored."[104] This wild space commands her attention, and that attention is a balm. The bubbles in the water "reminded her of the stars she had fallen in love with so long ago, years before she became an astronomer and began to spend her days analyzing solar data from the Yohkoh satellite or the RHESSI spectroscopic imager. The stars were no longer a mystery to her; these bubbles would have to do."[105] The prosaic natural world—for Jessica and for McGuane—is more of a mystery than the distant cosmos.

A comforting idea: that our earthly wilderness might eclipse the mysteries of space. When McGuane eloquently writes, "An important part of life, maybe the *most* important part, is the quest by each of us to discover something we believe to be more worthy and permanent than we are individually," it is possible that he is speaking not only of family and of writing but also of wilderness.[106] McGuane's interest in wilderness conservation "has really replaced any other kind of religious presence in my life"; it is "the sort of overarching spiritual presence of anything that I'm writing."[107]

He shares that sentiment with his longtime friend. Harrison and McGuane are able to find dangerous beauty in the wilderness without trite simplification. Harrison writes in one poem that "we are each / the only world / we are going to get"—a recognition of the wildness within and outside us.[108] That wildness, that wilderness, might be gentle and beautiful, but it carries an ancient power. When Harrison writes, "All the honest farmers in my family's past are watching / me through the barn slats, from the corncrib and hogpen. // Ghosts demand more than wives & teachers," he might as well speak of the patient ghosts of the wild.[109] Those ghosts thrive in thickets and rivers, in well-worn paths and open fields. They stir us most when we are open to them—and sometimes the gentle ritual of sustained attention is enough. The ghosts of the wild ask for respect and stewardship, and both Harrison and McGuane believe the wilderness has just demands.

5

A Tremendous Sublime

William Everson

In 1933, deep in California's Sequoia National Park, a young man named William Everson worked for the Civilian Conservation Corps. He spent eight-hour days "cutting a road to a fire lookout at the top of a peak."[1] The crew had no bulldozers, no jackhammers: only shovels and blasting powder. At twenty-one years old, it was Everson's "first prolonged experience of nature outside of the farmland" of his youth.[2]

Nearly thirty years later, a local television network airs a program about life at Saint Albert's, a Dominican priory near the University of California, Berkeley. The voice-over narrates: "Here, Brother Antoninus, who is a nationally known poet and a very famous fine printer, is printing some copies of his own poems on his hand press." The program features friars tending the garden, working in the woodshop, and chanting the Exsultet, an ancient Easter song of praise. Brother Antoninus, an apron over his black habit and his sleeves rolled past his elbows, nearly fades into the background of the black-and-white film. He holds up for the camera a section of long poetic lines spanning the page. Later in the program, he stands with the choir at the solemn Mass.

Brother Antoninus and Everson were one and the same. An ardent disciple of influential poet Robinson Jeffers, Everson was likewise a poet of nature and passion, rooted in the California wilderness. He spent nearly twenty years as a Dominican lay brother, a period that defined his life as a poet and that remains one of the most fascinating interludes of religious transformation in American poetry. Everson is a paradox: a religious poet torn between the sensuality of faith and liturgy and his own sexual desires. He embraced a monastic existence, then became an itinerant preacher of poetry—a "beat friar" who was profiled in *Time* magazine and who traveled across the country giving spoken word performances—only to end his religious life in one dramatic moment. Wilderness and religious faith defined his poetry and life; he was truly a poet of the literal and metaphorical wild, one who longed to capture its beautiful sublime.

Dana Gioia, California's former poet laureate, has appreciated Everson's work since 1977, when Stanford's literary magazine, of which Gioia was the poetry editor, published an issue devoted to Everson. "He is the archetypal West Coast bohemian intellectual," Gioia told me. "He could never have happened in the East—from farm to federal camp to bohemia to monastery to university to rural hermitage."

Everson was born in 1912 and raised on a farm in the San Joaquin Valley. His parents were Christian Scientists, although that biographical footnote is complicated. His father was agnostic in practice; his mother was born and raised Catholic, but the church wouldn't allow her to marry a divorced man. They were both printers who had met while working for a small newspaper in Minnesota before heading west. Their mix of residual Catholicism and pastoral agnosticism created a unique religious background for Everson.

But the young Everson wasn't pious. His first religious experience happened in October 1934 while attending Fresno State, when he discovered Jeffers's strange, visceral poetry. Jeffers's poems are sweeping odes to the value and violence of the natural world. His long, tumbling lines are Whitmanesque but wholly Californian in tone. In Everson's introduction to the reissue of Jeffers's *Cawdor and Medea* (1970), he writes that Jeffers's poetry represents how "the latent American pantheistic seed had found its Californian fertility."[3] Everson calls Jeffers "God-tormented,"[4] a man out of place in the Modernist era, whose "resilient, massive, intellectually resonant verse idiom . . . enabled him to assail with such authority the complacencies of his time."[5]

Everson later said that "Jeffers showed me God in the cosmos, it took and I became a pantheist."[6] Everson "knew where I was going to find Him—before my very eyes, as He is bodied forth in prime Nature. . . . The place was California, the Coast. I saw that He was intensely, incredibly alive in my own region."[7] Jeffers inspired Everson to create a God out of nature—the wilderness that surrounded him.

Inspired, he left college and returned to his hometown of Selma, about two hundred miles equidistant between San Francisco and Los Angeles, and married Edwa Poulson, whom he'd known since high school. They started a small vineyard, and Everson wrote poetry. From his earliest work, Everson was consumed with divinity and the wilderness. In "But There Was No Lament," a man disappears into the woods, without any context: "He walked through the waist-high wheat / And vanished in the woods."[8] His astonished family stared "at the somber trees."[9] It is a fitting way to understand Everson's embrace of the wilderness as a place of transformation.

His early vision of God is found there, but it is not yet a Christian God. In "Circumstance," Everson's description is rather pagan: "He is a god who smiles blindly, / And hears nothing, and squats faun-mouthed on the wheeling world, / Touching right and left with infinite lightning-like gestures. / He is the one to pray to, but he hears not, nor sees."[10]

In other poems, nature itself carries the whisper of divine. In "Odor of Autumn," that feeling is atmospheric: "That hold, like tawny wine, all summer's hauteur; / Over the hazy draws and the pine-thicket knolls, / Drifts the unmistakable odor of autumn."[11] His early writing is most charged when he describes the palpable, wild world: "And the earth bears. Back of the house / The blackberry riots the fences, swarms the tree, / Hiding the fruited runner under its thorn. / The apple, loosened, launches the long way downward, / Marked in its passage by the leaf's whicker. / All through the hovering deadness of the night / They give, go down."[12] They are the lines of a poet steeped in nature. And yet Everson, as time progressed, became skeptical that nature alone could satisfy him. Near the end of one long poem, "Late October '39," the narrator confesses, "This poem is the word of a religious man, with no god to worship."[13]

During these years, Everson self-published three collections: *These Are the Ravens* (1935), *San Joaquin* (1939), and *The Masculine Dead* (1942), books that the poet and editor Kenneth Rexroth helped Everson collect into *The Residual Years*. The two poets met shortly after Everson moved to the Bay Area in 1946. Rexroth was an anthology-minded poet (he edited the *New British Poets* anthology for New Directions). According to biographer Lee Bartlett, Rexroth invited Everson to an apartment party with the renowned critic and editor Cyril Connolly, during which Rexroth told the partygoers that "Everson is truly autochthonous. You won't find in him the Modernist touchstones by which we others go about what we do. He doesn't need our sophistication because he possesses a primal innocence; he doesn't need our ideas because he thinks through his skin and suffers through his thought."[14] Rexroth's long, anonymous blurb for *The Residual Years* makes even grander claims, calling Everson's poetry "simple, sensuous, and passionate, as Milton said great poetry should be."[15] Rexroth found Everson to be much like the poetry of those early volumes: pastoral, purely Californian, and more inclined toward nature than humanity, exactly the qualities Everson had appreciated in Jeffers.

Meanwhile, unrest in the wider world impacted Everson's California utopia. In the summer of 1942, Everson was asked to defend his request to not be drafted. His response brought together wilderness and faith: "The war caught me in the last phase of the intense state of religious feeling common at one time or another to young men. With some individuals that feeling finds its mode in the orthodox forms of religious practice. I, who had never received a thorough Christian training, found it in a response to Nature. It seemed to me that everywhere I might turn my eyes I beheld in the tangible forms of the natural world the illumination of a divine and benevolent Being."[16] Albert Gelpi, a longtime professor at Stanford whose scholarship has shaped understanding of the poet, wrote that "Everson's pantheism made him a pacifist."[17] For Everson, "death and destruction in nature were part of the ecological cycle," but violence from human hands was unacceptable.[18] Everson was placed in a foresting camp for conscientious objectors in Oregon during the war years. Poulson moved to San Francisco. Their marriage didn't survive the separation.

In Oregon, Everson worked as a printer, an art he'd inherited from his parents. Growing up, he fed press and set type but "did not have any finesse with it."[19] Skilled printers at the Oregon camp mentored him, and he was able to return to his poetry.

Everson left the camp in July 1946 and soon after met Mary Fabilli, a Catholic poet and artist. They would marry in June 1948. Everson's pantheism was tired; his mystical and religious longing found muse and matter in Fabilli, who had recently made an earnest return to the faith of her youth. During this period, Everson wrote poetry and spent time with fellow poets Rexroth and Robert Duncan. He also attended Catholic Mass with Fabilli.

Everson was skeptical of the institutional church, which he described as "a monolithic, quasi-political organization which by exploiting certain weaknesses in collective human nature, was able to solidify itself, perpetuate itself in history . . . and I hated it."[20] Yet he'd fallen for Fabilli, and he inherited her interest in the art of the church. He was moved by her phonograph record of Gregorian chants that played when he wrote in the house on Saturdays. He called it a "tremendous sublime . . . there was being shaped a dimension and a context, a movement of life around sacramental norms which I had never experienced before."[21] Fabilli's faith was a "fabulous Latin beauty, this Latin sensitivity," Everson wrote.[22] "And physical, profoundly physical. The concrete, sensible dimension pervading her whole mode of life."[23]

Meanwhile, Fabilli "began to civilize"[24] Everson, much to the chagrin of Rexroth, who wanted "[Everson to be] kind of an Abraham Lincoln character," according to Everson, who added, "I was in a way the central hope for his beat generation."[25] Indeed, Rexroth considered Everson the prototypical beat: a man who had suffered and who had been "locked up for his convictions."[26] Everson even looked the part of a wilderness man in the city, with his Pendleton shirt, forester's coat, and a "big black Mennonite style hat."[27]

No more. Now Everson donned a sports coat. He cut his hair. He applied for a Guggenheim—and got it. Everson was becoming nationally known. James Laughlin at New Directions published *The Residual Years* in 1948. Everson, a notorious perfectionist with a printer's eye, was unhappy with the book's typography and even quibbled over Rexroth's effusive dust jacket blurb, which he thought would antagonize critics and reviewers.

The tension with Rexroth was displaced by more spiritual concerns. Intrigued by Fabilli's faith, Everson was starting to reconsider his vision of God—and the mystical elements of nature were a spiritual source for his poems: "And the city-pent man, / Hemmed, at last goes forth, / And finds that fragrance of earth / But more: that look, as of merely the thrust of grass / At a fenced line, / And all breaks open and blazes, / Dances there in a wild descant / At the tip of the sight."[28] Everson had read Augustine's *Confessions* and was intellectually stirred but eager for a more immediate spiritual experience of his own. At church with Fabilli, "in the mystery of the Mass," he "hoped to find what she had found, what the book had promised."[29]

He found it at Midnight Mass in 1948, at Saint Mary's Cathedral in San Francisco. Nuns had prepared Christ's manger with fir trees, and the smell took Everson back to the farm of his childhood. A poet interested in cultivating a personal mythos, Everson found comfort in his belief that Christ would not make him renounce his devotion to the natural world. While his wife knelt in prayer next to him, Everson spent the moments before Mass in reverie. He not only thought of the Incarnation but also "remembered all the wildernesses I had known, the measureless night, and sensed their plight out there, those primitives, those sheepherders, watching their beasts through the jackal-haunted blackness, huddling a blaze."[30]

That synthesis of pagan shepherd and Christ as shepherd stirred Everson. He went to the crib at the front of the church as "one more poor wretch, who had nothing to bring but his iniquities."[31] Whenever Everson struggled with his Catholic faith, even years later, he would think of the beautiful wildness that announces the beginning of Mass: "a kind of inner spontaneous coming-up, as a flock of birds of the fields, out of some inner instinctual thing, rises: the commonness of it, the mutual identity of the need, and this, the response to the need."[32] The latent pagan sexuality of his earlier life and verse now found a new vessel: religious faith. He would never be the same. His past conception of the wilderness as a region of unbridled desire now seemed shallow. Everson could now embrace both nature and faith as existing in sustained communion with each other.

A few days later, Everson drafted "The Uncouth." Lines from an early version of the poem were inspired by his vision at Mass: "The sheep moved, / And on that scant forage / Browsed fitfully, bleating."[33] Although Fabilli had inspired Everson's conversion, their marriage couldn't exist in the eyes of the church. (Fabilli had been married previously, and although Everson wasn't Catholic when he married Poulson, she was. As of 1984, Everson was still writing to the diocese to annul their marriage.) Everson and Fabilli separated, and he wrote of the experience in "The Falling of the Grain": "The summer burns and blazes, / The year begins its drouth. / I watch the one I nevermore / May kiss upon the mouth."[34] Fabilli brought Everson to faith, but "the next day was the Lord's. Beyond it / Rose the immitigable week of His great word, / Schismatic in our lives."[35]

The poem is equal parts explanation and lament. "We erred," Everson writes, "We sought in each / What only God can give."[36] A deeply confessional and often conversational poet, Everson wavers between confidence and confusion in his poem but ultimately concludes with purpose. He left his job at a university press and learned how to bind books. In April 1950, his marriage over and enamored of his new spiritual mission, he left Berkeley for Oakland, where he joined the Catholic Workers, the communitarian movement founded by Dorothy Day and Peter Maurin (Everson's poems later appeared in Day's *Catholic Worker* newspaper). Carroll McCool, a former Trappist monk in charge of the house, noticed Everson's intellectual approach to religion and advised him to pray ten rosaries a day. The pair walked around Lake Merritt together and up and down the city streets, praying.

Even in the city, Everson found a sacred wilderness. In the soft light of summer dusk, he would walk to "the Oakland estuary among the deserted factories and warehouses, and out among the silent piers."[37] The day's noise of machines was replaced with silence. Everson watched the water, where "gulls lifted their wings in a gesture of pure felicity. . . . My mind shot north up the long coast of deliverance, encompassing all the areas of my ancient quest, that ineluctable instinct for the divine—the rivermouths and the sandskirted beaches, sea-granite capes and bastions and basalt-founded cliffs—where despite all man's meanness a presence remains unspoiled, the sacred zone between earth and sea, and pure."[38] His poetic and spiritual sense formed by the forest, Everson longed for the wilderness in his urban space, and inspired by a Catholic sense to find God in all things, his eyes were newly opened.

Everson set up his handpress in a shed behind the Catholic Worker house. He printed *Triptych for the Living* (1951), with engravings by Fabilli, while under the spiritual direction of Father Osborn, a Dominican. The excitement of Everson's initial conversion had begun to fade. Feeling "dry" in his faith, he had another mystical experience at Mass when "out of the tabernacle came this dark ray."[39] He collapsed in the pew and wept. He thought a struggle of the soul was inevitable when it came to faith: "I do believe that the life of God cannot be got through without crisis."[40]

Although taken by the Catholic Worker's tradition of tending to the poor, Everson longed for a more monastic existence. Everson chose the Dominicans because he could openly be a poet and a printer there. In May 1951, Everson joined Saint Albert's as a lay brother. The order's provincial chose the name of Brother Antoninus for Everson.[41] From his monastic room at Saint Albert's, Everson could see the "myriad glitter, uncountable" of San Francisco.[42] In the outside world, the "torque toward mere mechanical unity intensifies," Everson wrote, rebuking a world that is "scanting the vision of a transcendent God etched on the heart of man."[43] Everson thought of the professors and students at Berkeley and concluded, "I, a friar, musing in my cloister, who had only to move through the life of secular learning to find it not whole, have turned in here to a deeper integration."[44]

Ever the Jeffers disciple, Everson considered Saint Albert's more of a resort than a monastery. He "wanted it set in otherwise denuded earth, with one of those unforgettable Spanish crucifixes dominating the center."[45] He felt like "an utter anachronism, with my fake medieval attitudinizing in a modern cloister."[46] A parish priest who came to the annual retreat at the monastery quipped that Everson was "Ephrem the Deacon," a fourth-century saint.[47]

It was then that Everson met another Dominican named Antoninus—Father Antoninus Wall, a San Francisco–born priest ordained in 1950, who first clothed Everson in his habit during the poet's vestition ceremony at the priory. Father Wall was taken with Everson's seriousness and thought he would be a good choice to speak with theology students at the nearby Dominican School of Philosophy and Theology, which Everson did in 1958. The speech had a "tremendous impact" on the students, Wall told me, adding, "I've been sixty-eight years a priest, and it was still the most memorable talk of my entire priesthood that I've ever heard."[48] Everson gave the story of his conversion, including the mystical experience at Christmas Eve Mass the decade before.

The poems Everson wrote during his first years of conversion, 1949 to 1954, were later collected in *The Crooked Lines of God* (1959). Truly, to borrow the language of Gerard Manley Hopkins, Everson thought the world was charged with the grandeur of God, explaining in the book's foreword that the "matchless God-writing, calligraphed unendingly on trees, peaks, rivers, oceans, lakes, rebukes and dazzles me."[49] The poems are idiosyncratic and gushing paeans to his spiritual journey. Some, such as "Gethsemani," are glutted with majestic imagery and unite Everson's pre-Catholic sense—a sexual, natural primitivism—with his singular vision of God. Desire gives in to destiny here, for "whatever the flesh may suffer / The soul suffers before."[50] Everson envisions himself as a messenger, a man who traded the wilderness for monastic walls so that others could see "that the god was man, / That the man could faint, / This the world must know."[51]

Jesus's vulnerability appealed to Everson. The title "Gethsemani" refers to the garden in Jerusalem where Jesus and his disciples prayed. It was there that Judas found and betrayed Jesus with a kiss on the cheek, and the Passion narrative begins. "Is this the dream," Everson writes, "that God must dream in man?"[52] There is anger in Everson's lines, mirroring the frustration of the biblical narrative. Jesus was sent to "help redeem their fall," yet the disciples, seemingly "the best of humankind / Snore by the wall."[53]

"The Massacre of the Holy Innocents," another poem in the collection, is narrated by one of King Herod's soldiers who was sent to kill infant boys near Bethlehem. The soldier's monologue is as cold as the "land lay naked under a frost"; he and the men move from home to home in slaughter.[54] The narrator laments his guilt and the grief that followed. "No matter what dreams of grandeur /

Ennobled our sleep on the straw ticks of our barracks, / History stood by our side and said: these are the ones."[55]

Other poems laud the natural wild elements of Christ's cross: "Rough fir, hauled from the hills. And the tree it had been, / Lithe-limbed, wherein the wren had nested, / Whereon the red hawk and the grey / Rested from flight."[56] This natural sense becomes a refrain in the incantational poem "Passion Week," which begins, "Christ-cut: the cedar / Bleeds where I gashed it."[57] "The Holy Ghost / Gusted out of the sky / Aghast," Everson intones: "Bleed cedar. / Little cedar, / Lanced, / Axe-opened, / The ache of sacrifice."[58] For Everson, the best way to make Christ real was to stress his physical, pained body—that body on the wooden cross.

The Crooked Lines of God is an indictment of humankind and a work seared by the emotional charge of conversion. Everson's earlier work from *The Residual Years* feels like another world by comparison. Before his religious years, the prototypical Everson poem was one like "Noon," in which the natural world is absolute and awe inspiring: "The wind down, hushed; / In the sudden suspension of time and all motion / The sun lies heavily on the hand."[59]

Everson's admirers expected similar lines in his new work, but the natural God-consciousness of Jeffers had been replaced with Christ. James Dickey, reviewing Everson's book in the *Sewanee Review*, found the new book disappointing and argued that it even soured Everson's early poetry. For Dickey, rather than being cinctured by the habit of religious orthodoxy, Everson had finally found his staid form. Dickey's missive made it to Saint Albert's, and Everson responded, resulting in a series of posturing letters between the two poets that the *Sewanee Review* printed in full. Everson was clearly miffed. Piety had not pried away his ego. "Theologically," Everson counters, "it is not possible to over-stress a divine mystery. . . . That Mr. Dickey is ignorant of the theological and spiritual issues behind

Christian poetry is apparent, and really no fault of his, but it is not intelligent of him to indict what he does not understand."[60] When Everson wrote those letters, he was years estranged from the words he defended. Between 1954 and 1960, Everson underwent several crises of faith. For many, belief ebbs and flows, but Everson's shifts were especially acute. His faith struggles were personal, emotional, and intellectual—a tempest that surprised even his peers. Wall recalls that Everson once left Saint Albert's for three weeks when they brought in a television, which he saw as a symbol of modernity destroying their monasticism. Such seriousness suggests that Everson had become enamored of his own legend.

By the time he wrote those letters—in which he compares himself to Milton as well as to Isaiah and Jeremiah—Everson had become even more of a national figure. Cloaked in full habit, with a religious escort, he performed poetry readings and lectures in Chicago, Detroit, and other cities but was rebuked by then archbishop John Mitty, who preferred a quiet Everson, plying away on the handpress in solemn Saint Albert's.

Mitty's death in 1961 freed Everson to tour again, and he was especially drawn to colleges: Boston College, Purdue, Notre Dame, and Harvard, where he told the *Crimson* that he wrote poetry because "it is painful, but there will be a catharsis, a healing, and an appeasement."[61] He would arrive a few days early on a campus "to start some things moving, stir up some ferment . . . [and then] try to crest that by the reading night," as Wall recalls: "Wherever Everson went, he would try to absorb the spirit of the place, and try to become something like an oracle."[62]

Everson was not there to preach. He kept it literary and considered his readings "more encounters" than traditional lectures. Wall told me that once Everson signed with Naomi Burton—Thomas Merton's literary agent—he charged more than $1,000 for each reading, which meant the smaller Catholic colleges could no longer afford him. His audiences became ever more secular.

National Educational Television filmed one such reading in 1966. Everson came after poet Michael McClure, whose reading ended with him roaring like a lion, eyes closed, in front of an actual lion. Everson is mostly shot on stage, in front of a crowd. He squints behind glasses; his voice rises and falls. He sometimes speaks from memory and at other times reads from a book. "I rise to meet that vision," he intones, reading from "A Canticle to the Waterbirds," which ends with lines that recall the wilderness vision of Hopkins: "Curlews, stilts and scissortails, beachcomber gulls, / Wave-haunters, shore-keepers, rockhead-holders, all cape-top vigilantes, / Now give God praise. / Send up the strict articulation of your throats, / And say His name."[63]

Everson continued to write new poetry during his touring years, although much of it revived themes and styles from his past work. *River-Root*, a long, highly sexual poem about lovers, was finished in 1957 but wasn't published until 1976, long after Everson's Dominican years. *The Hazards of Holiness* (1962), although published upon completion, contains work that more closely mirrors his early verse, although he replaced folkloric evil spirits of the wilderness with the devil. "All the way to heaven / Is Hell," he writes in a poem titled after that first line, "And the devil posts it." The entire poem is a lament of temptation: "Oh, brother-devil! / Shadow and adversary! / My keeper! / Double of the heart's imago! / I do acknowledge!"[64]

Longing suffuses his work during this period. "You, God" is a plea to the divine: "My brain / Burns on your pierce. / My blood splits. / I shriek each nerve. // God! // Suck me in!"[65] That poem, along with "I Am Long Weaned," begins with epigraphs from the book of Job, a narrative of suffering. *The Hazards of Holiness* is the work of a soul torn between celibacy and desire; Everson was clearly torn and tired, and his art was suffering.

Something had to give, and it soon did. In 1959, Everson met Rose Tannlund. Their intense friendship was the inspiration for *The Rose of Solitude* (1966). In the prologue, a monk leaves his desert wilderness hermitage and "re-enters the world."[66] In prayer at a basilica, he meets a woman who seeks confession; she admits her love for a priest. In the poems that follow, Everson's narrator embraces desire. His "problem is primal."[67] He is unsure if the woman who tempts him is the devil, God, or both. Everson's friendship with Tannlund and his writing of *The Rose of Solitude* mark a turning point in his evolving faith—he was forced to explicitly acknowledge the conflict between his religious devotion and his erotic sense. He began to imagine the possibility of leaving the priory.

In 1965, Everson met Susanna Rickson, an undergraduate at San Francisco State College. The full extent of this relationship was a secret—even to colleagues such as Father Wall. In the summer of 1969, he and Everson embarked on a trip to Europe. Wall was finishing his doctoral studies in Rome and thought it would be good for Everson to see the church's aesthetics and deep presence in Europe. Everson was in the process of attaining his final vows to become a priest.

Yet toward the end of their time in Europe, Wall had the strong sense that something was taxing Everson's mind. The poet was always looking for mail from Rickson, and in October, he returned to the United States. On December 7, 1969, Everson gave a reading at the University of California, Davis. He read "Tendril in the Mesh," which became the first poem of *The Integral Years*, the final work in his cumulative trilogy (which includes *The Residual Years* and *The Veritable Years*). Equal parts love and lust, the poem made clear Everson's plans: "Take down from your shoulders the silks that have baffled the sun."[68] He took off his Dominican robe and reportedly told the audience, "This is my habit, and when I take it off, I take off my own skin. But I have to take it off to find my heart."[69] Everson left the order. Six days later, he wed Rickson in a civil ceremony, in front of two witnesses: the publishers of Oyez Press, a Berkeley-based outfit that published several of Everson's later books.

Everson went on to publish poetry and prose after his religious years. He taught, continued printing, and took on a shamanic hue—an evolution via a Jungian system that started with instruction by a Dominican priest. Everson wrote that the shaman "goes out into the wilderness, yes, to gain his prophetic identity in solitude where his charismatic destiny is revealed to him."[70] Gone from the monastery walls, Everson believed our craving for the wilderness was a natural balance against civilization. "I think the world has a growing interest in wilderness," Everson said, "because, as the human race becomes more and more urbanized, the importance of wilderness is going to grow. The world's going to turn to the men who are the celebrators of wilderness for sustenance."[71] For Everson, the wilderness is the "archetypal American address, the archetypal American vision, the archetypal American fantasy. And that's the thing that counts. Reality can offer very little to stand against it."[72]

Years after Everson left the order, Father Wall invited him back to speak with students and told me that Everson seemed remorseful: "I gave up all of this for the sake of a woman."[73] There was something at the core of the monastic life that Everson—who remained a Catholic and was buried in a Dominican cemetery—could never give up. Bill Hotchkiss, a friend of Everson, said that when the poet was among nature, deep in the forest or next to a stream, he would say, "Forgive me," as if speaking to God for leaving the monastery.[74] A man driven and swayed by his passions, Everson was a religious seeker who never appeared satisfied unless he was stirred by uncomfortable faith. He found that blessed discomfort in Catholicism, in poetry, and most often, in the wilderness, which seemed the purest version of God. He sought ways to name and capture that divine sublimity, but it escaped him.

In declining health from Parkinson's disease, Everson died at his home in Santa Cruz on June 3, 1994, at the age of eighty-one. Catholic, pantheist, friar, lover—Everson embraced the paradoxes and myths of his life, but he was most purely a seeker of faith in the wilderness. A line from a 1962 letter best captures his identity: "My archetype has been the solitary visionary who isolates himself in nature and views the concerns of man from afar."[75] Everson's poetry was powerful and particular—the work of a man shaped by the California wilderness. His vision of divinity evolved from a pantheistic, nebulous power source to a decidedly Christian God: a God whose complexity not only encompassed Everson's unique poetic vision of the wilderness but also transformed that vision into a tremendous sublime.

6

Salvific Wilderness

Mary Oliver and W. S. Merwin

Thomas Merton often returned to the Desert Fathers and Mothers because their eremitic lives were devoted not to asceticism itself but to asceticism as an act "of submission and cooperation with God's will."[1] The wilderness enables and cultivates this bodily journey to spiritual knowledge because that search for gnosis "is a response to the will of God for the restoration of the cosmos to its primitive state."[2] In order to find what we seek, we must return, pare back, escape.

Merton, like so many others, realized that faith in the wilderness was a journey, not a location of answers. The wilderness grows and grows and dies and moves; it resists our desire for stasis and understanding. The wilderness itself, then, becomes an apt metaphor for belief: it is neutered when it nears certainty. To have faith in the wilderness means to accept that it is untouchable even when grasped.

However tenuous our relationship with the wilderness, with enough humility—of the eremitic or ascetic kind, or otherwise—the wilderness serves a salvific function. The wilderness saves poets and prophets in various ways. It is a comfort, a balm, a source of necessary confusion. Its expanse expands us. For Mary Oliver and W. S. Merwin—two of the most renowned contemporary American poets—the salvific nature of the wilderness sustained their art and their worldviews. Although their styles and subjects differed, they were activists for the wild: they believed a return to the wilderness was not merely necessary but inevitable. The wilderness is our true, ancient home.

A few months before she would turn twenty-eight, Oliver—secretary for the sister of the esteemed late poet Edna St. Vincent Millay—published a poem in the *Massachusetts Review*. "How I Went Truant from School to Visit a River," an ode to ditching school in favor of the woods, sits in the back of the volume. Later that year, Oliver would publish her first of nearly twenty books of poetry. She would go on to win the Pulitzer Prize and the National Book Award and become crowned the country's best-selling poet—by a landslide. Yet no matter how far her star rose, she always went back to that river. She always went back to the woods.

Popularity is a blessing and burden in the world of poetry. The art form is cultivated in those little magazines—often released to little acclaim and few readers. Oliver's life as a poet began in those pages, but she rose to dizzying levels of popularity, and her ascent came with a cost. Her detractors mistook fluidity for simplicity, sincerity for sentimentality. Oliver was a poet of the woods, and the woods are a place where we can't help but admit the world's mystery and beauty.

Years later, reflecting on the subject of that early poem, Oliver explained that she would head to high school but take a detour "most mornings into the woods instead, with a knapsack of books."[3] She read Walt Whitman there and soon fell in love with two "blessings—the natural world, and the world of writing: literature."[4] She "felt at ease" in the woods: "Nature was full of beauty and interest and mystery, also good and bad luck, but never misuse."[5] The natural world's "otherness"—its peculiarity, its singularity—"is antidote to confusion," and entering that wild world "can re-dignify the worst-stung heart."[6]

From her youth to the final years of her life, Oliver's faith was in a familiar wilderness. She did not long for vast expanses or deep journeys. "I am dazzled not so much by what I have never seen before, but by what I have never noticed before," she wrote.[7] "Someone else might prefer raw wilderness, something new or strange. But I need the same old proving ground. I don't want the sight before me to change, only the depth of my looking."[8]

Oliver was born to look. "I am patient as a stone and stubborn as crabgrass," she affirmed.[9] Rather than heading into the world with ideas, she took the inverse approach: "It is from the particulars of the world that the mind begins its abstracting, thinking process."[10] Her poems came from watching and wondering—not from the will. She needed the woods, not in theory, but in footfall and feeling.

As a young child in Maple Heights, Ohio, Oliver would always walk upstream rather than downstream. She recalled how the "water pushed against my effort, then its glassy permission to step ahead touched my ankles. The sense of going toward the source."[11] Oliver was always drawn to that spiritual origin: "Something is wrong, I know it, if I don't keep my attention on eternity."[12] Her path was one not of philosophy or theory but instead of experience. She returned to a desire "to be lost again" so that she could reach creation—an action that required her to touch the wild world, her "face into the packets of violets, the dampness, the freshness, the sense of ever-ness."[13]

Any poetic or creative aspiration that Oliver held—as a young secretary beginning to publish or as a famous poet in the twilight of her career—was inspired by her belief that the natural world was her spiritual home. "I am not talking about having faith necessarily, although one hopes to," she wrote.[14] "What I mean by spirituality is not theology, but attitude."[15] This attitude was a tendency to accept the miraculous nature of the world as a constant, not an anomaly.

Such a vision began during her childhood years in Ohio—years Oliver later revealed were not idyllic but rather marred by suffering—and continued to her adult life in New England. Oliver lived in Provincetown, Massachusetts, with her partner, the photographer Molly Malone Cook. She wrote of walking along the water in that town, where she "was able to see the earth not as our reckless ambitions have rearranged it, but as it was created by those infinitely more mysterious forces: wind, storm, time."[16]

Oliver's faith in the wilderness meant succumbing to those forces. She accepted that she would give her body "back, someday, without bitterness, to the wild and weedy dunes."[17] She believed that was her—our—destiny: "Soon enough, we are lambs and we are leaves, and we are stars, and the shining, mysterious pond water itself."[18] Before she returned to that dust from whence she came, though, Oliver pledged a selfless ars poetica. Her vision of the poet's responsibility was wholly natural: "Before we move from recklessness into responsibility, from selfishness to a decent happiness, we must want to save our world."[19] Yet in order to save the world, Oliver thought we must first be saved by it—we must acknowledge and embrace the salvific nature of the wilderness.

That requires us to "become familiar with it again," to slow down, step into the woods, and breathe the air.[20] "That is where my work begins, and why I keep walking, and looking," a poetics of humble observation.[21] Oliver's precise and patient descriptions of small pockets of wilderness—the forest at town's edge, the strip of trees separating properties, a quiet and secluded shore—offer her readers a liturgy of observation. Great writers of the wild can help us better see so that we might go back to those spaces with a closer sense of texture.

Oliver embraced solitude in the wild as a way to clear the mind and the ears: "For me it was important to be alone; solitude was a prerequisite to being openly and joyfully susceptible and responsive to the world of leaves, light, birdsong, flowers, flowing water."[22] Her most acute method of prayer was alone in the woods. "If you have ever gone to the woods with me," she wrote in one poem, "I must love you very much."[23] "I will hear some sound of the morning as it settles upward," she writes, listening to "the rustling of a flock of snow buntings, high and wild in the cold air, like seeds, rushing toward me, and then away."[24]

In one essay, Oliver wrote of leaning forward and looking down into a pond, that "mirror of roughness and honesty—it gives back not only my own gaze, but the nimbus of the world trailing into the picture on all sides."[25] Her choice of "nimbus" is perfect here: the world's fine edges are blurred, trees and bodies blossoming into each other in a grand synthesis of nature. As Oliver stares into the water, her gaze focusing on herself, the water, the world, she sees the reflection of swallows darting across the pond, and in the mirror of the water, the birds "are flying therefore over my shoulders, and through my hair."[26] Even the turtle that "pauses slowly across the muddy bottom" touches her reflected body.[27]

There is a sense of Hopkins's inscape here. We are changed by nature, but perhaps our soul and spirit engage the world as well—a communal affirmation. In "Picking Blueberries, Austerlitz, New

York, 1957," the prototypical Oliver poem, the narrator falls asleep during the summer among the blueberries, and she wakes "when a deer stumbled against me."[28] They share a moment, silent except for the wind, before the deer bounds away—"but the moment before she did that / was so wide and so deep / it has lasted to this day."[29]

Oliver suggests that if we want to be amazed, we need to pay attention and see what exists around us as innately new. One theme consistent in this recognition is a Hopkinsesque transformation, settling into the world. She demonstrates this idea in "Drifting," when she describes being half-asleep, moving through the world as if in a dream. "I didn't intend to start thinking about God, / it just happened."[30] God might be invisible, but "holiness is visible."[31] We shouldn't mistake Oliver's nature-inclined spirituality for the pantheism of early William Everson. Oliver recognizes the sacral nature of the wild world, but she envisioned God as encompassing and transcending the literal nature before her.

Prayer—in the wilderness and through the wilderness—is a refrain for Oliver. "I know a lot of fancy words," she wrote in "Six Recognitions of the Lord."[32] "I tear them from my heart and my tongue. / Then I pray."[33] In that same poem, she calls on the Holy Spirit directly, with the "fragrance of the fields and the / freshness of the oceans which you have / made, and help me to hear and to hold / in all dearness those exacting and wonderful / words of our Lord Christ Jesus, saying: *Follow me*."[34] In other poems, nature's wildness becomes psalmic: "Glory / to the rose and the leaf, to the seed, to the / silver fish. Glory to time and the wild fields, / and to joy. And to grief's shock and torpor, its near swoon."[35] In "Sometimes," she prays, "God, rest in my heart / and fortify me, / take away my hunger for answers."[36]

Oliver's faith in the wilderness comes from her assertion that wisdom and transcendence are found there—a consistent vision from her earliest to final poems. *Devotions*, her selected works, was arranged by Oliver's latest poem to her earliest, a decision that reflects some measure of consistency and clarity in her life. One of the newer poems, "This Morning," is about redbird chicks who chirp for food. "As to anything else, they haven't / had a single thought," she writes, "Their eyes / haven't yet opened, they know nothing / about the sky that's waiting."[37] The narrator thinks how the birds don't even realize their future, impossible gift of flight—and in her plain-spoken yet precise language, Oliver concludes, "And just like that, like a simple / neighborhood event, a miracle is / taking place."[38]

Her narrators reflect Oliver's desire to be enfolded by the wilderness. Without the comfort of the forest, they feel incomplete. "All my life," one narrator speaks, "I have been restless— / I have felt there is something / more wonderful than gloss— / than wholeness— / than staying at home."[39] The ecstatic pull toward nature comes from the heart, not the mind. It is incantational— "yes, I am willing to be / that wild darkness, / that long, blue body of light."[40] In Oliver's poem "White Flowers," the narrator ponders her mortality and falls asleep, where she dreams of "that porous line / where my own body was done with / and the roots and the stems and the flowers / began."[41]

This union between body and nature and between mind and imagination feels like the inevitable trajectory of our life among the wilderness. Our inevitable return to the ground should not be seen as an end-of-life event alone. We might ponder her work as a lifetime of preparation, a cultivating ritual of return. How much more inviting might eternity feel if we imagine the wilderness as its lasting symbol, the place where we might find comfort in the inevitable. When the character in the poem "Peonies" rushes outside into a garden and grabs white and pink flowers from the ground, she feels "their honeyed heaviness, their lush trembling, / their eagerness / to be wild and perfect for a moment, before they are / nothing, forever?"[42] Oliver's sense of inscape extends Hopkins's conception of our relationship to the wild, reaching near symbiosis.

Merwin longed for a similar communion with the wild, but the tone and style of his vision differed. Born in New York City in 1927, Merwin grew up in Union City, New Jersey, where his mother read him a book about Native Americans who lived deep in a forest, and he told her, "I like the idea of living with trees all around me."[43] His father, William Stage Merwin, was the minister of First Presbyterian Church, "a tall, yellow-brick, turn-of-the-century structure, with two steeples, a rose window, and green carpets down the sloping aisles."[44] Merwin remembers his rather stern father occasionally taking him to the study upstairs of the church. While his father worked on his sermon, Merwin stared out the window, "watching the [Hudson] river, without a word, utterly rapt in the vast scene out in front of me, hearing my father muttering words of scripture ('Thou fool, this night shall thy *soul* be required of thee') somewhere far behind me."[45] He watched trains "crossing the river on railroad ferries, all shades of orange in the sunlight. White puffs of steam climbed out of unseen whistles and horns, the distant sounds arriving, faint and faded, a long breath afterward. I was seeing something that I could not reach and that would never go away."[46]

The church itself had seen better days. The building had begun to weather, and attendance was sparse. Yet young Merwin listened raptly to his father "reading the psalms and reading the Bible from the pulpit. And I was fascinated by the language. I was fascinated by hearing the psalms."[47] He would draw pictures while his father intoned from the pulpit, and something in the kinesthetic experience cemented the moment: Merwin "knew a lot of the King James Version of the Bible from my father's reading—just by heart, without even thinking about it. That was a different kind of English that rang in my ear. And I was very fond of it."[48]

Merwin did not inherit his father's Christian faith. Although fascinated by the person of Jesus, Merwin would later be drawn to Buddhist practice. Yet he did carry something from those days spent in that old city church: "an urge to love and revere something in the world that seemed to me more beautiful and rare and magnificent than I could say, and at the time in danger of being ignored and destroyed."[49]

For young Merwin, the wilderness was foreign—and tenuous. Other than glimpses in literature, the closest he had gotten to the wild natural world was a trip to the country. After that, he began "to have a secret dread—and a recurring nightmare—of the whole world becoming city, being covered with cement and buildings and streets. No more country. No more woods."[50] As he became older, Merwin was drawn to Henry David Thoreau's idea of wildness and "the recognition that the human can not exist independently in a natural void."[51]

Merwin found other classic American writers lacking in their depictions of humans and the wilderness. He admired Whitman but thought "his rhetorical insistence on an optimistic stance, [could] be quite wonderful as a statement of momentary emotion, but as a world view and as a program for confronting existence it bothered me when I was eighteen and bothers me now."[52] He thought Whitman's tendency to talk about "the American expansion and the feeling of manifest destiny in a voice of wonder" revealed a crucial problem: in Whitman's "momentary, rather sentimental" poetic view, Native Americans as well as buffalo and other "species that are being rendered extinct" become wiped out "as though they were of no importance. There's a cultural and what you might call a specietal chauvinism involved."[53]

The American West is a symbol of these concerns for Merwin. Similar to Everson and Terry Tempest Williams, Merwin thought the West to be "a landscape of the imagination."[54] Those who have lived in the West have an image of that place "traversed and overlaid with hopes and hearsay, rumors from the immense sage of wishes and awe, endurance and loss, that keeps rising from the unknown continuing life of the place."[55] For someone like Merwin, a poet born and raised in the Northeast, who has only visited the West, "what we remember has glowed in absence like enormous figures held on a screen."[56]

Here the artifice of his imagery and language is telling. Merwin's earliest conception of wilderness spaces was created through story and art. The wilderness was always consistent with myth, and yet Merwin thought myth "is something like the intuition of a kind of coherent sense of experience, which we can't live without. But it is our own projection. It is real in the sense that it's necessary. To us."[57] This is the trick—or perhaps the ultimate gift—of the wilderness. It is both myth and purest reality. It seems as if it is too beautiful or raw to exist, and yet it is existence incarnate.

Merwin has told an anecdote about the poet Robert Bly, who said that there was surrealism in Merwin's poems—about flies moving in circles "around a statue of nothing."[58] Merwin took Bly into a room on his farm "and showed him flies going round and round and round in a circle, in the middle of the room."[59] We seek meaning and structure, and when they are not apparent, we project them. We seek to explain, for then we are present among the indifferent wilderness: we matter. The natural, wild world seems supernatural from a distance. This paradox creates ample tension for writers and artists. Returning to Merwin and the West—a place of wilderness that was his only through imagination—that American vastness was "heroic in an incredibly cramped and vicious way. People did suffer and were magnificent, but they were also broken and cruel, and in the long run incredibly destructive, irreversibly destructive. What we've done to this continent is something *unbelievable*—to think that one species could have done this in a hundred years."[60]

Merwin struck these chords as early as the 1970s. "We are living in a world surrounded by human contraptions instead of living creatures," Merwin lamented, "and I profoundly believe this is something that can't go on. I don't think we can live in a completely human-made world."[61] He feared living in a "completely fabricated world" and felt "our destruction of other species is disastrous to our own minds."[62]

In 1976, a few years after he won his first of two Pulitzer Prizes for poetry, Merwin moved to Hawai'i, where he studied Zen Buddhism with Robert Aitken Roshi. It is best to understand Merwin as—at least outwardly—existing with the Zen lineage of literature rather than spiritual practice. Merwin was "extremely chary" about the latter, saying, "I don't think of this as some dazzling discovery that completely changed my life. I think that finding certain writings of Zen, or of Buddhism, seemed to confirm something that I had been reading toward for years."[63] Merwin's literary Buddhism was the culmination of an intellectual and emotional route that started with the lyric but distant King James Bible coming from his father—a man he feared but would later come to respect, with resignation, and a man who was both distant and familiar to him—and was supported by Merwin's interpretation of how the natural world was historically perceived. He has spoken of the pre-industrial world's "anxiety creeping in about the connection with nature" and the resulting "animism underlying mythology" of the Renaissance.[64] He thought such animal-human-world synthesis could be overdone, but "Shakespeare certainly understood it. Look at *As You Like It*. And you know, a figure like Prospero, in *The*

Tempest, is a sort of summary of all that. The magic is all there. It's not something spooky that is supernatural. It's natural."[65]

Here it helps to consider Merwin as a Zen Buddhist whose worldview was formed in a Protestant-Christian sphere. "I'm not a Christian but I think Jesus was an amazing occurrence on the planet and I think we've made of him something that he never was or ever wanted to be,"[66] Merwin reflected. "But there are incredible things that he said," including the Lukan representation of Jesus's words that "the kingdom of heaven is within you."[67] Although Merwin criticized some traditional Christian approaches toward wilderness, he was not in opposition to the religion. He was interested in transcendence and synthesis. "Take them away, names like Buddhism," Merwin concluded. "I'm impatient with them. There's something beyond all that, beneath all that that, they all share, that they all come from. They are branches from a single root. And that's what one has to pay attention to."[68]

Merwin paid attention to that spiritual, wild root in his poetry—and through his life in Hawai'i. He lived with his wife, Paula, on a three-acre section of a former pineapple plantation, where they worked on "trying to grow and save endangered species of trees and plants."[69] Hawai'i was a microcosm of Merwin's vision of the wilderness: an isolated space that could be gently brought back to its premodern state. The area had been deforested in the mid-nineteenth century, and Merwin "always wanted to take a piece of ruined land and to see if I could bring it back to life again . . . to un-ruin it."[70] His ambitious idea to "restore Hawaiian rain forest" proved to be a real challenge.[71] They planted hundreds of koa trees and many 'ōhi'a trees, but most died, "either by the change in the soil or by the insects that had never been here when the Hawaiians were here."[72]

The flora and fauna of Hawai'i "had almost all evolved there. There's no other place on earth where this is true. There is still no place on earth which is as priceless a laboratory for studying evolution as the Hawaiian Islands, and they have been raped and torn apart by large-scale exploitative agriculture."[73] That destruction prompted Merwin to become an ardent activist, lobbying those in the writing community to pressure the American government to protect the rain forests of Hawai'i. In a 1989 letter to the *American Poetry Review*, which was reprinted elsewhere, Merwin writes that many are aware of the destruction of the earth's vast, iconic rain forests, but "few, in any state, are currently aware that there is a tropical lowland rain forest within what is now politically the United States, and that it is presently in danger of disappearing even more rapidly than the forests of South America and southeast Asia."[74] Construction machines had begun to "gouge" into the Wao Kele O Puna forest, an area known for native flora and one of the places where native birds, "wiped out everywhere else in the lowlands, have managed to survive."[75] 'Ōhi'a trees "were smashed, cut up, and buried in crushed lava."[76] Streams that crossed the land "were interrupted, filled with mud and weed seeds from the huge tires."[77]

Eventually, Merwin's passionate activism and determined cultivation resulted in what would later be called the Merwin Palm Forest, eighteen acres of a protected wet palm forest at the Pe'ahi Stream on Maui's north shore. Merwin's dream to be surrounded by trees finally came true, and he was able to return life to a place that had nearly lost it. Merwin realized that "what are called concerns—for ecology and the environment, for example—merge inevitably with work done every day, within sight of the house, with our own hands, and the concerns remain intimate and familiar rather than abstract and far away."[78]

Merwin's habitual work in the garden and forest is an affirmation of his spiritual connection to the land. The island was a fitting metaphor of mortality for him: there is only so much space to move, so much air to breathe before we leave this world. His poetry journeys along similar routes, seeking to describe the wilderness song as our inevitable hymn—much like Oliver, he creates poems in which his narrators are drawn to nature, our best possible chance at an eternal soul. "From having listened absently but for so long," Merwin writes, "It will be the seethe and drag of the river / That I will hear longer than any mortal song."[79]

We must be humble in order to meet and receive the wilderness, to hear its song. There is a slight mysticism to some of Merwin's work; mysticism is where wilderness enters his senses. His poem "Finding a Teacher" feels much like a fable: the tale of a narrator going into the woods and finding an old friend who was fishing. The narrator asks him a question, and the man tells him to wait instead. The narrator's question was "about the sun // about my two eyes / my ears my mouth / my heart the earth with its four seasons."[80] His question, ultimately, was about life. There was no need to answer; the asking itself was the answer. A Buddhistic sentiment is reflected in other pieces where absence becomes presence, as in "Provision": "I will take with me the emptiness of my hands / What you do not have you find everywhere."[81]

Nature and time are also connected for Merwin. In "Dew Light," the narrator walks through his garden, thinking that "when the news about time is that each day / there is less of it," and "only the day and I are here with no / before or after."[82] The narrator of another poem wonders how stars hold our desires and dreams night after night, "How it was that we traced / In their remote courses not their own fates but ours."[83]

Despite the grandness of the cosmos and the relative majesty of the wilderness, Merwin's life as a curator of his small space of the world—how he was able to restore the land itself back to health—is reflected in the resigned optimism of "Place." "On the last day of the world / I would want to plant a tree," the narrator says, so that its roots would reach the water beneath the surface.[84] The modern world—our lives—might end, but the wilderness will remain. He ends the poem with great pacing: "And the clouds passing // one by one / over its leaves."[85]

The poetry of Oliver and Merwin, although syntactically distant from the bounding rhythms of Gerard Manley Hopkins, share his duality of joy and melancholy. Perhaps that is how we most authentically encounter the wilderness. To see the wilderness fully and wholly, we must humble ourselves. Quiet and patient, we feel the forest's invitation, and yet our physical communion is temporary. Like others who have faith in the wilderness, Oliver and Merwin know the wilderness will outlast us, and our machines, and our ambitions.

Merwin has written about the places "that once had been forest and had grown back / into a scrubby wilderness alive with / an earthly choir"—the wild world thrumming with crickets, birds, voles, rabbits, foxes, and the wind.[86] Both poets knew they would join the wilderness soon enough, so their collected work becomes the preparation for an elegy. Oliver and Merwin show that the wilderness can be salvific; rather than a place to be tamed, it is a raw source of the divine. Eternity awaits; the wilderness is our saving preparation.

Conclusion

A Clearing in the Wilderness

"It's late night already," the German philosopher Martin Heidegger wrote in 1926; "The storm is sweeping over the hill, the beams are creaking in the cabin, life lies pure, simple, and great before the soul."[1] The six- by seven-meter cabin was built for Heidegger in 1922 in Todtnauberg, a village in the Black Forest. Surrounded by trees, it is built into the slope, leading into the valley below. A hillside spring filled the well that faced Heidegger's study window, the flow a steady song.[2]

Other than his home in the city, the mountain hut was the philosopher's main space for writing, including the composition of *Being and Time*. He could hear the thrilling storms that seemed to shake the mountain, and by day, he would venture out for walks where "the meadows and pasture lands lead to the woods with its dark fir-trees, old and towering."[3] This was his "work-world."[4] "On a deep winter's night," he explained, "when a wild, pounding snowstorm rages around the cabin and veils and covers everything, that is the perfect time for philosophy. Then its questions must become simple and essential."[5]

Heidegger thought his philosophical work was like that of the herdsman, the farmer, the peasant. He had little time for fellow academics. Philosophy might be an intellectual activity, but it was also elemental, and the "struggle to mold something into language" felt much like "the resistance of the towering firs against the storm."[6] One needed the wilderness for such experiences. "In large cities one can easily be as lonely as almost nowhere else," but Heidegger instead craved solitude, which "has the peculiar and original power not of isolating us but of projecting our whole existence out into the vast nearness of the presence of all things."[7]

His time on the mountain—days walking on paths in the woods and nights writing while wind and water filled the sky—likely influenced one of his core philosophical tenets. For Heidegger, much of our lives are redundant and uninspired. But sometimes, in the midst of that rote existence, "an open place occurs. There is a clearing, a lighting."[8] Much of Heidegger's complexity as a thinker is owed to his idiosyncratic semantics and terminology, yet his decisions were always deliberate, and on this metaphorical point, he was clear to focus on nature. "The forest clearing (opening) is experienced in contrast to dense forest, called 'density' (*Dickung*) in older language," he wrote, and this "clearing, the opening, is not only free for brightness and darkness, but also for resonance and echo, for sounding and diminishing of sound."[9]

For Heidegger, we find ourselves in the wilderness, particularly when we are in a clearing within that wilderness—where the wild surrounds us but does not subsume us. The result is a comfort through discomfort: a transformation in which we humble ourselves, and that clearing grants "access to the being that we ourselves are."[10] We need the wilderness for creation; we need the wilderness to live.

The idea of the clearing in the wilderness precedes and transcends Heidegger—and all of his troubling worldviews on other subjects—yet his formulation of the concept is useful. It offers us a way to place and orient humans in the wild while affirming the integrity of those wild spaces. Its spiritual element reflects some vestiges of his Catholic childhood in the Black Forest, when Heidegger's father was a sexton at the local church and young Martin and his brother were servers. Heidegger briefly studied toward the priesthood at the Jesuit seminary in Freiburg and then left Catholic practice, but he retained a nostalgic vision of his Catholic youth.

His description of that religious time carries a similar texture as his vision of the clearing: "The mysterious fugue in which the church feasts, the days of vigil, and the passage of the seasons and the morning, midday, and evening hours of each day fitted into each other, so that a continual ringing went through the young hearts, dreams, prayers, and games—it is this, probably, that conceals one of the most magical, most complete, and most lasting secrets of the [church] tower."[11]

The mysterious sensuousness of religious ritual evolved or perhaps was perfected in the wilderness. Later that century, and across the ocean, an American writer would offer a vision similar in concept but different in subject. By 1988, Toni Morrison was already a distinguished novelist, but her book *Beloved* led to recognition that culminated in her receipt of the Nobel Prize in Literature several years later. *Beloved* envisions the wilderness as a space for resurrection and danger.

The novel begins at and largely takes place within the house at 124 Bluestone Road in Cincinnati, Ohio—a house made claustrophobic from haunting. A mischievous and sometimes violent ghost harasses Sethe (a formerly enslaved person) and her daughter, Denver. Sethe is reunited with Paul D, who was enslaved with her at the Sweet Home plantation. "I got a tree on my back," Sethe tells Paul D shortly after he arrives.[12] Paul D comes behind and embraces her, drawn to her wound: "She straightened up and knew, but could not feel, that his cheek was pressing into the branches of her chokecherry tree."[13]

Her body, whipped and scarred, survives through a metaphor of wilderness. When she dreams of her sons, Howard and Buglar, gone from 124 for fear of the haunting, she imagines them "sometimes in beautiful trees, their little legs barely visible in the leaves."[14] When Beloved—the mysterious apparition of the child Sethe killed years earlier—arrives at 124, she "walked out of the water."[15]

Beloved is not the only one born in the wilderness in the story. Denver got her name from Amy Denver, a white indentured servant who helped a pregnant, fleeing Sethe years earlier. Denver was born in the Ohio River as "water sucked and swallowed itself beneath them."[16] The scene's spiritual inflection is apparent in Morrison's description: "On a riverbank in the cool of a summer evening two women struggled under a shower of silvery blue. They never expected to see each other again in this world and at the moment couldn't care less. But there on a summer night surrounded by bluefern they did something together appropriately and well."[17] Both Denver and Beloved were born of the wilderness and are miraculous in their own way.

Yet it is another character, Baby Suggs, who most powerfully encapsulates Morrison's spiritual vision of the wilderness. Sethe's mother-in-law, Baby Suggs, is first introduced in the novel with a note that she has died—and yet her absence in the book feels like presence. The clearing is a central place of wilderness in the novel and perhaps the perfect Morrison symbol: an affirmation of spirituality amid suffering. The clearing is where, in the past, "Baby Suggs had danced in sunlight."[18] Heidegger's conception of the clearing is eerily present here: the implication of light as consistent with the space of the clearing. "This open center is therefore not surrounded by what is," Heidegger writes, "rather, the lighting center itself encircles all that is, like the Nothing which we scarcely know."[19] By existing only within the past narrative of the novel, Baby Suggs becomes a preternatural force: in some ways, a typology for both Sethe and Beloved. In Heidegger's conception, the perfect clearing of ourselves is best imagined "as the forest free of trees at one place"[20]—a designation through absence. The wilderness crafted.

Baby Suggs had "become an unchurched preacher, one who visited pulpits and opened her great heart to those who could use it."[21] She would preach in churches during the fall and winter, and then when "warm weather came, Baby Suggs, holy, followed by every black man, woman and child who could make it through, took her great heart to the Clearing—a wide-open place cut deep in the woods nobody knew for what at the end of a path known only to deer and whoever cleared the land in the first place."[22]

They would congregate each Saturday afternoon there, and Baby Suggs "sat in the clearing while the people waited among the trees."[23] She prays and then calls for them: children, men, and then women, who enter this clearing within the wilderness and dance and pray. Her preaching was not to tell them "to clean up their lives or go and sin no more. She did not tell them they were the blessed of the earth, its inheriting meek or its glorybound pure. She told them that the only grace they could have was the grace they could imagine."[24]

In the church of the wilderness, imagination was transformative. All was possible, including a bending of time. Years later, struggling with her simultaneous embrace and fear of Beloved, Sethe longs to return to the clearing "before the light changed, while it was still the green blessed place she remembered: misty with plant steam and the decay of berries."[25] She goes there with Denver and Beloved "late one Sunday morning."[26] The clearing was now a nearly domesticated space, "big-city revivals were held there regularly now, complete with food-laden tables, banjos and a tent."[27]

Now Sethe sits on Baby Suggs's rock, "Denver and Beloved watching her from the trees."[28] She soon feels like Baby Suggs's ghost is trying to choke her. Was it Beloved? Does it matter there, in the clearing, where Sethe might finally be open to the truth of this nightmarish resurrection? In Morrison's novel, the spirit of the clearing leaves the physical wilderness and becomes the communal power of women—those who come to rid 124 of Beloved, as the troubling stories about her powers begin to spread. When women arrive at the house to drive the mysterious Beloved away, Sethe grabs her hand and stands with her in the doorway: "For Sethe it was as though the Clearing had come to her with all its heat and simmering leaves, where the voices of women searched for the right combination, the key, the code, the sound that broke the back of words."[29]

The women become the wilderness itself, as their communal song rises to become "a wave of sound wide enough to sound deep water and knock the pods off chestnut trees. It broke over Sethe and she trembled like the baptized in its wash."[30] Beloved, like the spirit she is, disappears. Yet her presence, like memory, remains: "Down by the stream in back of 124 her footprints come and go, come and go."[31]

* * *

What if the wilderness itself is the clearing?

I've lived my entire life in New Jersey, the most densely populated state in America. Cars clog the parkway and the turnpike.

Apartments rise in cities, and developments cram suburbs. Beautiful parks, rivers, and lakes are scattered across my state, but a lot of people means a lack of privacy. Yet there is almost a mythical—or perhaps supernatural—wilderness here: the Pine Barrens. John McPhee, a fellow native son of the Garden State, wrote, "The picture of New Jersey that most people hold in their minds is so different from this one that, considered beside it, the Pine Barrens, as they are called, become as incongruous as they are beautiful."[32] Yet as McPhee notes, the Pine Barrens "are so close to New York that on a very clear night a bright light in the pines would be visible from the Empire State Building."[33] This wilderness is home to an especially strange bit of folklore.

Only one professional sports team is named after a three-hundred-year-old devil. When the Colorado Rockies moved to New Jersey in 1982, they traded mountain peaks for the boggy swamps surrounding the Brendan Byrne Arena and needed a new nickname. Local newspapers ran a contest, and more than ten thousand fans chose the nickname Devils, named after my state's strange legend.

Deep in the Pine Barrens—a densely forested, mossy, and marshy swath that seems like another country compared to the state's suburbs, cities, and shore points—lies the birthplace of the Jersey Devil. In 1735, Mother Leeds was pregnant with her thirteenth child and suffered terrible labor. She called for help from the devil and finally gave birth to a boy. Yet the child soon transformed into a beast, with horns, wings, and talons, its body covered in thick, dark hair. The devil killed its family and then escaped through the chimney, wreaking havoc in the New Jersey backwoods until this day.

Like all good legends, this one has its share of twists and turns. Mother Leeds was a descendent of Daniel Leeds, a Quaker turned almanac publisher, whose son got in a feud with the one and only Benjamin Franklin. Franklin penned some particularly nasty rumors about the Leeds family, which might have evolved into the legend of the devil. Franklin isn't the only historical figure associated with the legend. Former King of Spain Joseph Bonaparte—Napoleon's brother—reported a sighting of the devil during a hunting trip.

The Jersey Devil is often mischievous, known for dancing on fences and leaving hoofprints on snowy roofs, but he occasionally returns to the violence of his birth. He's caused some real damage, ransacking farms and attacking dogs, chickens, and livestock. During one hellish spate of sightings in 1909, factories and schools closed. Reports have become infrequent, but he remains a tale told by older generations.

It's a tale that has spooked and intrigued so many New Jersey kids—including me. Because New Jersey is so densely populated, so thoroughly and inescapably modern in its development, there remains a deep longing for the strange. It's no surprise that one of the most popular homegrown publications in the state is *Weird NJ*: a compendium of true and fabricated tales of eccentricities and horrors. There's a reason almost every New Jersey suburb has a "spot," a thin strip of woods that everyone has a story about.

By spring break of my senior year of high school, my friends and I had trekked to every folklore spot in our county: haunted railroad tracks, Revolutionary War graveyards, and old farms where someone swore they could hear a child's whistle in a barn. What suburban kids like us really wanted, though, was the authentic wilderness, a place of lore a little bit to the south. In the last weeks of Lent, we chose an unusual pilgrimage. We drove down the muggy state parkway in a minivan whose speedometer froze at twenty-five and reached Little Egg Harbor, where we rented a flat campsite next to a river, the only people around on a Wednesday afternoon in late

March. We grilled hamburgers and steaks before heading out into the trails armed with a camcorder and too much ambition.

Our expedition through the swampy, mossy land turned up nothing—not a feather, not a bone, not a snout, not a footprint—but we couldn't leave empty-handed. We promised a story, so we made one up. We waited until midnight and then drove down the campsite's empty oval roads. Rocks churned beneath our tires, and I held the searchlight out the window, sweeping the woods. One of my friends sprinted from behind a tree, and the shaking camcorder caught his ominous outline in the dark.

Years later, I wonder why I remember that errant afternoon so well. Why do I remember that the campsite cost eight dollars or that our potato chips were stale? Why can I still hear the whistle of the hastily arranged tent snapping in the wind? I remember because the wilderness holds stories like nowhere else. And in a world where wilderness is becoming increasingly ignored, decimated, and forgotten, even our foolish expeditions into the wild take on some significance.

W. S. Merwin, Mary Oliver, Toni Morrison, Jim Harrison, William Everson, Gerard Manley Hopkins, and the other writers, poets, and philosophers in this book do not share a unified vision of the wilderness because the wilderness rejects classification, for its taxonomy is not ours. The best we can do is approximate our relationship to that world. Rick Bass, chronicler of life in the Yaak region of Montana, thinks there is "some third, mysterious thing, between us and the imagination, between our landscape (internal or external) and our imagination."[34] That third, mysterious thing might be called "spirit."[35]

Following Bass, is "spirit" the *feeling* of being in the wilderness or the wilderness itself? The activist Edward Abbey, during his time as a park ranger near Moab, Utah, at the Arches National

Monument, wasn't sure what we mean by *wilderness*. "The word itself is music," Abbey feels, and although we "scarcely know what we mean by the term," the mere "sound of it draws all whose nerves and emotions have not yet been irreparably stunned, deadened, numbed by the caterwauling of commerce, the sweating scramble for profit and domination."[36]

For Abbey, the word *wilderness* "suggests the past and the unknown, the womb of earth from which we all emerged. It means something lost and something still present, something remote and at the same time intimate, something buried in our blood and nerves, something beyond us and without limit."[37] He quotes the French playwright Honoré de Balzac, who observed, "In the desert there is all and there is nothing. God is there and man is not."[38] The sentiment initially seems opposed to the eremitic revelations of the Desert Fathers, although it captures the necessary and inevitable distance between us and the wilderness. Abbey concludes that the desert "is as it is and has no need for meaning. The desert lies beneath and soars beyond any possible human qualification. Therefore, sublime."[39] Sublime and distant. Near the end of *Desert Solitaire*, his consideration of the desert wilderness of Utah and beyond, he is "convinced now that the desert has no heart, that it presents a riddle which has no answer, and that the riddle itself is an illusion created by some limitation or exaggeration of the displaced human consciousness."[40]

To name the wilderness—to map it, to sing of it, to attempt to save it—is to place a human vision upon that which is wild. "Who defines the natural world for us?" the essayist Barry Lopez wonders. "Who decides the names of things?"[41] Most importantly, "How do we conceive of the natural world? As having a nonhuman purpose? As being 'therapeutic' or 'beautiful and enriching' and therefore useful?"[42] For even in *saving* the wilderness, we so often envision that salvation as of utility to us. We destroy, we have mercy, we save. We, not the wilderness.

The British novelist John Fowles wrote of this quandary in *The Tree*. As a boy, living forty miles from London, he remembers his father's small, cramped garden with "five orchard apple trees, kept manageable only by constant debranching and pruning."[43] In contrast to his father's stern, provincial management, Fowles's uncle and cousins spent time in nature. Soon, the boy "secretly craved everything our own environment did not possess: space, wildness, hills, woods . . . I think especially woodland, 'real' trees."[44]

When he was able to own property himself, he rejected his father's tendency toward control: "I must confess my own love is far more of trees, more exactly of the complex internal landscapes they form when left to themselves."[45] He feared naming and classification, which he thought "destroys or curtails certain possibilities of seeing, apprehending and experiencing."[46] To name trees—or the wilderness—means "attempting to own them."[47] This might seem like a cynical view. Wasn't his fellow countryman Hopkins drawn to writing and sketching the flora he encountered on walks? And when that natural world arrived in his poems, it was illuminated and not neutered.

The Tree, appropriately enough, blossoms as it develops. Fowles qualifies his earlier stance, stern in its own way: "I discovered, too, that there was less conflict than I had imagined between nature as external assembly of names and facts and nature as internal feeling; that the two modes of seeing or knowing could in fact marry and take place almost simultaneously, and enrich each other."[48] What Fowles believes is most important is being absolutely present in the moment of the wilderness—to embrace "its seeming transience, its creative ferment and hidden potential."[49] He describes one particular spot, Wistman's Wood: "But it is the silence, the waitingness of the place, that is so haunting; a quality all woods will have on occasion."[50]

It might seem cold comfort to have faith in something that is beyond us and without limit. Yet the wilderness forces us to reconsider what we desire of it—what we expect of the natural world. The wilderness, plainly, humbles us. Its beauty, its vastness, its fragility, and its eventual resurrection: the wilderness is beyond us and not for us. I think of Robert Macfarlane's description of climbing the summit of Ben Hope. There at night, he feels strange. The place was "entirely, gradelessly indifferent" to his presence.[51] "Up there," he reflects, "I felt no companionship with the land, no epiphany of relation like that I had experienced in the Black Wood."[52] He is correct that "all travellers to wild places will have felt some version of this, a brief blazing perception of the world's disinterest. In small measures it exhilarates. But in full form it annihilates."[53]

We have been broken by lesser forces than the wilderness. The wild world demonstrates to us, as Fowles says, the "inalienable otherness of each, human and non-human, which may seem the prison of each, but is at heart, in the deepest of those countless million metaphorical trees for which we cannot see the wood, both the justification and the redemption."[54]

The justification and the redemption: that which we are and which saves us. That spirit permeates *Laudato si'*, the 2015 encyclical from Pope Francis. The title means "praise be to you" and is taken from a canticle by Saint Francis of Assisi. The encyclical has the subtitle *On Care for Our Common Home*—a statement of communion. Right from the start, following in the tradition of Brazilian theologian Leonardo Boff, the encyclical connects the plight of the poor with the suffering of the planet: "The violence present in our hearts, wounded by sin, is also reflected in the symptoms of sickness evident in the soil, in the water, in the air, and in all forms of life. This is why the earth herself, burdened and laid waste, is among the most abandoned and maltreated of our poor."[55]

Francis thinks the wild earth demands our attention. He is direct here: the plight of the world is our fault. "Saint Francis," he writes, "faithful to Scripture, invites us to see nature as a magnificent book in which God speaks to us and grants us a glimpse of his infinite beauty and goodness."[56] He chastises "some committed and prayerful Christians, with the excuse of realism and pragmatism, [who] tend to ridicule expressions of concern for the environment."[57] No better are "passive" believers who wish not to be inconvenienced by a change of habits.[58] What is needed, Francis argues, is an "ecological conversion" so that "the effects of their encounter with Jesus Christ become evident in their relationship with the world around them. Living our vocation to be protectors of God's handiwork is essential to a life of virtue; it is not an optional or a secondary aspect of our Christian experience."[59] The wilderness is a place for a Baptist, for a Messiah, and for us.

If we are to return to something more eternal than ourselves—if we are to discover it for the first time—then we must allow our faith in the wilderness to exist in the only way faith can, without our control. The clearings of the wilderness might offer us transcendence, but that does not make them ours. Hopkins, in lines that sound much like prayers, offers us wisdom on this point: "Let them be left, / O let them be left, wildness and wet; / Long live the weeds and the wilderness yet."[60]

Acknowledgments

Sections of this book previously appeared in different forms in *Rolling Stone*, Literary Hub, *The Millions*, the Poetry Foundation, and *National Review*; I appreciate the support of those editors.

Continuing gratitude to my parents. Many thanks to my editor, Emily King, and the entire team at Broadleaf Books.

Amelia, Olivia, and Jennifer: thank you for exploring forest trails with me and for being constant sources of wonder.

Notes

Preface

1 Wallace Stegner, "The Wilderness Letter," Wilderness Society, December 3, 1960, https://tinyurl.com/y5rgk4x8.

2 Stegner.

3 Stegner.

4 Stegner.

5 Paul Brooks, *The Pursuit of Wilderness* (Boston: Houghton Mifflin, 1971), 5.

6 Max Oelschlaeger, *The Idea of Wilderness* (New Haven, CT: Yale University Press, 1991), 14.

7 Roderick Nash, *Wilderness and the American Mind* (New Haven, CT: Yale University Press, 2001), xi.

8 Nash, xii.

9 John Muir, *Our National Parks* (Boston: Houghton Mifflin, 1902), 1.

10 Brooks, *Pursuit of Wilderness*, 212.

11 David Noel Freedman, ed., *Eerdmans Dictionary of the Bible* (Grand Rapids, MI: William B. Eerdmans, 2000), 1378.

12 George H. Williams, *Wilderness and Paradise in Christian Thought: The Biblical Experience of the Desert in the History of*

Christianity (Eugene, OR: Wipf and Stock, 2016), 4.

13 Ulrich Mauser, *Christ in the Wilderness: The Wilderness Theme in the Second Gospel and Its Basis in the Biblical Tradition* (Eugene, OR: Wipf and Stock, 2009), 14.

14 Williams, *Wilderness*, 12.

15 Isa 43:19–20.

16 Deut 32:10.

17 Ezek 34:25.

18 Matt 12:43.

19 Freedman, *Eerdmans Dictionary*, 1378.

20 Oelschlaeger, *Idea of Wilderness*, 61.

21 Dante Alighieri, *The Divine Comedy*, trans. Henry Wadsworth Longfellow (Boston: Ticknor and Fields, 1867), 1.

22 Oelschlaeger, *Idea of Wilderness*, 5.

23 Nash, *Wilderness*, 17–18.

24 William Wordsworth and Samuel Taylor Coleridge, *Lyrical Ballads and Other Poems* (Hertfordshire, England: Wordsworth Editions, 2003), 6–7.

25 Wordsworth and Coleridge, 7.

26 Raymond Williams, *Problems in*

Materialism and Culture (London: Verso, 1980), 72.

27 John Gatta, *Making Nature Sacred: Literature, Religion and Environment in America from the Puritans to the Present* (Oxford: Oxford University Press, 2004), 10.

28 William Cronon, ed., *Uncommon Ground: Rethinking the Human Place in Nature* (New York: W. W. Norton, 1995), 79–80.

29 William Wordsworth, *The Collected Poetry of William Wordsworth* (Hertfordshire, England: Wordsworth Editions, 1994), 289.

30 Wordsworth, 289.

31 Wordsworth, 289.

32 Wordsworth, 289.

33 Cronon, *Uncommon Ground*, 70.

34 Joy Porter, *Native American Environmentalism: Land, Spirit, and the Idea of Wilderness* (Lincoln: University of Nebraska Press, 2014), 3.

35 Porter, 5.

36 Porter, 7.

37 Vine Deloria Jr., *God Is Red: A Native View of Religion* (Golden, CO: Fulcrum, 1994), 60.

38 Deloria Jr., 67.

39 Ralph Waldo Emerson, *The Selected Writings of Ralph Waldo Emerson* (New York: Modern Library, 2000), 6.

40 Emerson, 6.

41 Monica Weis, *Thomas Merton's Gethsemani: Landscapes of Paradise* (Lexington: University Press of Kentucky, 2015), 142.

42 Thomas Berry, *The Great Work: Our Way into the Future* (New York: Harmony / Bell Tower, 1999), 17.

43 Thomas Merton, *When the Trees Say Nothing: Writings on Nature* (Notre Dame: Sorin, 2003), 17.

44 Merton, 18–19.

45 Gary Snyder, *The Practice of the Wild* (Berkeley, CA: Counterpoint, 1990), 16.

46 Melvin McLeod, ed., *The Best Buddhist Writing 2007* (Boston: Shambhala, 2007), 28.

47 Henry David Thoreau, *Walden and Other Writings* (New York: Modern Library, 2000), 298.

48 Thoreau, 298.

49 Susan Fenimore Cooper, *Rural Hours* (New York: Putnam, 1850), 187.

50 Cooper, 188.

51 Cooper, 188.

52 Berry, *Great Work*, 55.

Introduction

1   Williams, *Wilderness*, 10.

2   Williams, 10.

3   Mauser, *Christ*, 27.

4   Mauser, 21.

5   Mauser, 22.

6   Mauser, 22.

7   Mauser, 36.

8   Mauser, 36.

9   Williams, *Wilderness*, 13.

10 Mauser, *Christ*, 15.

11 1 Sam 24:3.

12 1 Macc 2:27.

13 1 Macc 2:29.

14 1 Kgs 19:4.

15 1 Kgs 19:8.

16 Isa 35:9.

17 Isa 51:3.

18 Marco Rotman, "The Call of the Wilderness: The Narrative Significance of John the Baptist's Whereabouts" (PhD diss., Vrije Universiteit Amsterdam, 2019) 59.

19 Rotman, 59.

20 Jack Finegan, *The Archeology of the New Testament: The Life of Jesus and the Beginning of the Early Church* (Princeton, NJ: Princeton University Press, 1992), 3.

21 Luke 1:39.

22 Luke 1:42.

23 Luke 1:76.

24 Luke 1:80.

25 Finegan, *Archeology*, 6.

26 Finegan, 6.

27 Paul Burns, *Butler's Lives of the Saints: August* (London: Burns & Oates, 1995), 300.

28 Mark 1:6.

29 James A. Kelhoffer, *The Diet of John the Baptist: "Locusts and Wild Honey" in Synoptic and Patristic Interpretation* (Tübingen, Germany: Mohr Siebeck, 2005), 5.

30 Kelhoffer, 9.

31 Matt 11:18.

32 Kelhoffer, *Diet*, 29.

33 Kelhoffer, 98.

34 Kelhoffer, 120.
35 Robert H. Gundry, *Matthew: A Commentary on His Literary and Theological Art* (Grand Rapids, MI: William B. Eerdmans, 1982), 45.
36 Gundry, 122.
37 John P. Meier, *A Marginal Jew: Rethinking the Historical Jesus*, vol. 2 (New York: Doubleday, 1994), 22.
38 Mark 1:7.
39 Meier, *Marginal Jew*, 35.
40 Dale C. Allison, *Constructing Jesus: Memory, Imagination, and History* (Grand Rapids, MI: Baker Academic, 2010), 205.
41 Kelhoffer, *Diet*, 126.
42 Meier, *Marginal Jew*, 27.
43 Kelhoffer, *Diet*, 127.
44 Meier, *Marginal Jew*, 20.
45 Meier, 20.
46 Meier, 20.
47 Rotman, "Call of the Wilderness," 184.
48 Mark 6:20.
49 Mark 6:20.
50 Mark 6:26.
51 Mark 6:16.
52 Kelhoffer, *Diet*, 149.
53 Daniel Sheerin, "St. John the Baptist in the Lower World," *Vigilae Christianae* 30 (1976): 1–22.
54 Kelhoffer, *Diet*, 150.
55 Kelhoffer, 158.
56 Kelhoffer, 169.
57 Paul Burns, *Butler's Lives of the Saints: February* (Collegeville, MN: Liturgical, 1998), 34–35.
58 Burns, 34.
59 Eric Marshall White, "Albrecht Altdorfer's Botanical Attribute for Saint John the Baptist," *Notes in the History of Art* 15, no. 2 (Winter 1996): 15.
60 White, 15.
61 John 5:35.
62 White, "Albrecht Altdorfer's Botanical Attribute," 18.
63 Richard Bernheimer, *Wild Men in the Middle Ages: A Study in Art, Sentiment, and Demonology* (Cambridge, MA: Harvard University Press, 1952), 2.
64 Bernheimer, 8.
65 Bernheimer, 12–13.
66 Bernheimer, 13.
67 F. J. Foakes Jackson and Kirsopp Lake, trans., *The Beginnings of Christianity. Part 1. The Acts of the Apostles* (London: Macmillan, 1933), 433.
68 Jackson and Lake, 433.
69 Jackson and Lake, 435.
70 Jackson and Lake, 434.
71 Jackson and Lake, 434.
72 Jackson and Lake, 20.
73 Burns, *Butler's: February*, 102.
74 Burns, 102.
75 Meier, *Marginal Jew*, 100.
76 Mark 1:11.
77 Mark 1:13.
78 Mark 8:27.
79 Kelhoffer, *Diet*, 125.
80 Meier, *Marginal Jew*, 169.
81 Meier, 169.
82 Meier, 132–133.
83 Meier, 176.
84 Williams, *Wilderness*, 23.

Chapter 1

1   William Harmless, *Desert Christians* (Oxford: Oxford University Press, 2004), 82.
2   Henri Nouwen, *The Way of the Heart: The Spirituality of the Desert Fathers and Mothers* (New York: HarperOne, 1981), 27.
3   Richard Rodriguez, *Darling: A Spiritual Autobiography* (New York: Penguin, 2014), 19.
4   Rodriguez, 26.
5   Rodriguez, 29.
6   Rodriguez, 47.
7   Rodriguez, 216.
8   Deut 8:15–16.
9   Freedman, *Eerdmans Dictionary*, 340.
10 Freedman, 340.
11 Matt 4:1–2.
12 Mark 1:13.
13 Freedman, *Eerdmans Dictionary*, 340.
14 Matt 14:13.
15 John 6:14.
16 John 6:15.
17 Thomas Merton, *A Course in Desert Spirituality*, ed. Jon M. Sweeney (Collegeville, MN: Liturgical, 2019), 3.
18 Nouwen, *Way of the Heart*, 13.
19 Nouwen, 14.
20 Thomas Merton, *The Wisdom of the Desert* (New York: New Directions, 1970), 4.
21 Nouwen, *Way of the Heart*, 15.

22 Nouwen, 15.
23 Merton, *Wisdom*, 6.
24 Merton, 7.
25 Merton, 13.
26 Merton, 14.
27 Merton, 14.
28 Merton, 16.
29 Merton, 20.
30 Nouwen, *Way of the Heart*, 69–70.
31 Merton, *When the Trees*, 168.
32 Thomas Merton, *Disputed Questions* (New York: Harcourt Brace, 1985), 191.
33 Merton, *When the Trees*, 162.
34 Merton, *Disputed*, 191.
35 Merton, 198.
36 Thomas Merton, *Zen and the Birds of Appetite* (New York: New Directions, 1968), 117.
37 Harmless, *Desert*, 412.
38 Benedicta Ward, *The Sayings of the Desert Fathers* (Trappist, KY: Cistercian, 1975), 37.
39 Ward, 157.
40 Nouwen, *Way of the Heart*, 25.
41 Harmless, *Desert*, 401.
42 Harmless, 401.
43 Thomas Merton, *No Man Is an Island* (New York: Harcourt Brace, 1955), 106.
44 Merton, *Disputed*, 210.
45 Merton, 224–225.
46 Merton, *Zen*, 129.
47 Matt 19:21.
48 Harmless, *Desert*, 62.

49 Harmless, 65.
50 Gustave Flaubert, *The Temptation of Saint Anthony*, trans. Lafcadio Hearn (New York: Modern Library, 2001), xiv.
51 Flaubert, xiv.
52 Flaubert, xiv.
53 Flaubert, xii.
54 Flaubert, xxi.
55 Flaubert, xxxi.
56 Flaubert, xxv.
57 Flaubert, xxiv.
58 Flaubert, xxviii.
59 Flaubert, 9.
60 Flaubert, 9.
61 Flaubert, 10.
62 Flaubert, 12.
63 Flaubert, 13.
64 Flaubert, 34.
65 Flaubert, 34.
66 Flaubert, 35.
67 Flaubert, 52.
68 Flaubert, 170.
69 Flaubert, 170.
70 Flaubert, 191.
71 Flaubert, 191.
72 Merton, *Wisdom*, 21.
73 Merton, *Disputed*, 84.
74 Flaubert, *Temptation*, 87.
75 John Climacus, *The Ladder of Divine Ascent*, trans. Colm Luibheid and Norman Russell (Mahwah, NJ: Paulist, 1982), 75.
76 Merton, *Disputed*, 85.
77 Merton, 166.

Chapter 2

1 Gerard Manley Hopkins, *The Collected Works of Gerard Manley Hopkins*, vol. 3, *Diaries, Journals, & Notebooks*, ed. Lesley Higgins (New York: Oxford University Press, 2015), 617.
2 Gerard Manley Hopkins, *The Sermons and Devotional Writings of Gerard Manley Hopkins*, ed. Christopher Devlin, SJ (London: Oxford University Press, 1959), 262.
3 Hopkins, *Diaries, Journals, & Notebooks*, 617.
4 Gerard Manley Hopkins, *The Collected Works of Gerard Manley Hopkins*, vol. 4, *Oxford Essays and Notes*, ed. Lesley Higgins (New York: Oxford University Press, 2006), 50.
5 Gerard Manley Hopkins, *Poems and Prose*,

ed. W. H. Gardner (Baltimore: Penguin, 1968), 3.
6 Hopkins, 4.
7 Margaret Bottrall, ed., *Gerard Manley Hopkins: Poems, a Casebook* (London: Macmillan, 1975), 150.
8 Gerard Manley Hopkins, *The Journals and Papers of Gerard Manley Hopkins*, ed. Humphry House (Oxford: Oxford University Press, 1959), 23.
9 Hopkins, 23.
10 Hopkins, 24.
11 Hopkins, 57.
12 Hopkins, 57.
13 Hopkins, *Poems*, 91.
14 Hopkins, 109–110.
15 Hopkins, *Journals*, 127.
16 Hopkins, 130.

17 Hopkins, 175.
18 Hopkins, 180.
19 Hopkins, 179.
20 Hopkins, 181.
21 Bottrall, *Gerard Manley Hopkins*, 202.
22 Hopkins, *Journals*, 196.
23 Hopkins, 196.
24 Hopkins, 204.
25 Hopkins, 199.
26 Hopkins, 205.
27 Hopkins, 215.
28 Hopkins, 215.
29 Hopkins, *Poems*, 121.
30 Hopkins, *Journals*, 220.
31 Hopkins, 219.
32 Hopkins, 227.
33 Hopkins, *Poems*, 27.
34 Hopkins, 27.
35 Hopkins, 27.
36 Hopkins, 27.
37 Gerard Manley Hopkins, "Easter Sunday: Gerard Manley Hopkins," U.S. Catholic, March 27, 2016, https://tinyurl.com/y5ob936m.
38 Hopkins.
39 Hopkins, *Poems*, 28.
40 Hopkins, 30.
41 Hopkins, 31.
42 Hopkins, 31.
43 Gerard Manley Hopkins, *The Letters of Gerard Manley Hopkins to Robert Bridges*, ed. Claude Colleer Abbott (London: Oxford University Press, 1955), 66.
44 Hopkins, 66.
45 Bottrall, *Gerard Manley Hopkins*, 31.
46 Bottrall, 39.
47 Bottrall, 39.
48 Bottrall, 40.
49 Bottrall, 128.
50 Hopkins, *Poems*, 31.
51 Hopkins, 31.
52 Hopkins, 64.
53 Hopkins, xxii.
54 Hopkins, 65.
55 Hopkins, 38.
56 Hopkins, 38.

57 Hopkins, 54.
58 Hopkins, 55.
59 Hopkins, 32.
60 Hopkins, *Journals*, 200.
61 Hopkins, 200.
62 Hopkins, 242.
63 Hopkins, 50.
64 Hopkins, *Letters to Bridges*, 73.
65 Hopkins, 69.
66 Hopkins, *Journals*, 200.
67 Robert Bernard Martin, *Gerard Manley Hopkins: A Very Private Life* (New York: HarperCollins, 1992), 203.
68 Hopkins, *Journals*, 230.
69 Hopkins, 230.
70 Gerard Manley Hopkins, *The Correspondence of Gerard Manley Hopkins and Richard Watson Dixon*, ed. Claude Colleer Abbott (London: Oxford University Press, 1955), 75.
71 Gerard Manley Hopkins, *The Collected Works of Gerard Manley Hopkins*, vol. 7, *The Dublin Notebook*, ed. Lesley Higgins and Michael F. Suarez, SJ (New York: Oxford University Press, 2014), 36.
72 Hopkins, *Poems*, 50.
73 Hopkins, 50.
74 Hopkins, 50.
75 Hopkins, 50.
76 Hopkins, 50.
77 Hopkins, 50.
78 Hopkins, *Letters to Bridges*, 46.
79 Hopkins, 46.
80 Hopkins, 303.
81 Hopkins, 303.
82 Hopkins, *Poems*, 68.
83 Hopkins, 68.
84 Hopkins, 68.
85 Hopkins, 68.
86 Hopkins, *Correspondence with Dixon*, 157.
87 Hopkins, *Poems*, 68.
88 Hopkins, 68.
89 Hopkins, 68.
90 Gerard Manley Hopkins, *Selected Poems*, ed. Bob Blaisdell (New York: Dover, 2011), xxxiii.

Chapter 3

1 Terry Tempest Williams, *A Voice in the Wilderness: Conversations*, ed. Michael Austin (Logan: Utah State University Press, 2006), 169.
2 Thomas Merton, "The Wild Places," *Catholic Worker* 34, no. 3 (June 1968): 4.
3 Terry Tempest Williams, *Refuge: An Unnatural History of Family and Place* (New York: Vintage, 2018), 192.
4 Williams, *Refuge*, 193.

5 Thomas Merton, *Monks Pond: Thomas Merton's Little Magazine* (Lexington: University Press of Kentucky, 1968), 269.

6 Merton, "Wild Places," 4.

7 Merton, *When the Trees*, 63–64.

8 Merton, 161.

9 Merton, "Wild Places," 4.

10 Merton, 4.

11 Merton, 4.

12 Merton, 4.

13 Merton, 4.

14 Merton, 4.

15 Merton, 4.

16 Wendell Berry, *Essays 1969–1990*, ed. Jack Shoemaker (New York: Library of America, 2019), 597.

17 Berry, 597.

18 Berry, 597.

19 Wendell Berry, "The Unforeseen Wilderness," *Hudson Review* 23, no. 4 (Winter 1970–1971): 633.

20 Berry, 638.

21 Berry, 646.

22 Wendell Berry, *Conversations with Wendell Berry*, ed. Morris Allen Grubbs (Jackson: University Press of Mississippi, 2007), 41.

23 Berry, 58.

24 Berry, 96.

25 Berry, 96.

26 Berry, 4.

27 Berry, 133–134.

28 Wendell Berry, *This Day: Sabbath Poems Collected and New, 1979–2013* (Berkeley, CA: Counterpoint, 2013), xxi.

29 Wendell Berry, *Essays 1993–2017*, ed. Jack Shoemaker (New York: Library of America, 2019), 31.

30 Berry, 31.

31 Berry, 35.

32 Berry, 35.

33 Berry, 34.

34 Berry, *Essays 1969–1990*, 646.

35 Berry, 597.

36 Berry, *This Day*, 11.

37 Berry, 11.

38 Berry, 36.

39 Berry, 41.

40 Berry, 42.

41 Berry, 335.

42 Berry, *Conversations*, 161.

43 Berry, *This Day*, 65.

44 Berry, 120.

45 Berry, 187.

46 Berry, 187.

47 Wendell Berry, "Wild and Domestic," *Orion*, October 14, 2018, https://tinyurl.com/y7slrlmt.

48 Berry.

49 Berry.

50 Berry.

51 Terry Tempest Williams, "The Glorious Indifference," *Orion*, August 4, 2014, https://tinyurl.com/y548fdgj.

52 Williams, "The Glorious Indifference."

53 Jay Parini, ed., *The Oxford Encyclopedia of American Literature* (New York: Oxford University Press, 2004), 3:428.

54 Williams, *Voice in the Wilderness*, 22.

55 Williams, 169.

56 Williams, 169.

57 Williams, *Refuge*, 14.

58 Williams, 69.

59 Williams, 69.

60 Williams, 55.

61 Williams, 5.

62 Williams, 5.

63 Williams, *Voice in the Wilderness*, 39.

64 Williams, *Refuge*, 148.

65 Williams, 148.

66 Williams, 108–109.

67 Williams, 50.

68 Williams, 240.

69 Williams, *Voice in the Wilderness*, 18.

70 Williams, 23.

71 Williams, 23.

72 Williams, 23.

73 Terry Tempest Williams, *An Unspoken Hunger* (New York: Vintage, 1995), 48.

74 Williams, 48.

75 Terry Tempest Williams, *Red: Passion and Patience in the Desert* (New York: Vintage, 2002), 61.

76 Williams, 4.

77 Williams, 4.

78 Williams, 5.

79 Williams, 5.

80 Williams, 5.

81 Williams, 7.

82 Williams, 181.

83 Terry Tempest Williams, *Leap* (New York: Pantheon, 2000), 63.

84 Williams, 65.

85 Williams, 226.

86 Williams, *Red*, 7.

87 Terry Tempest Williams, *The Hour of the Land* (New York: Picador, 2016), 10.

88 Williams, 216.

89 Williams, 108.

90 Williams, 108.
91 D. H. Lawrence, *Lady Chatterley's Lover* (New York: Penguin, 1994), 323.
92 Williams, *Unspoken Hunger*, 57.
93 Williams, 57.
94 Berry, *Essays 1969–1990*, 258.
95 Berry, 259.

96 Berry, 259.
97 Berry, 259.
98 Berry, 331.
99 Berry, 332.
100 Berry, 332.
101 Berry, 332.
102 Williams, *Voice in the Wilderness*, 99.

Chapter 4

1   Thomas McGuane, *Conversations with Thomas McGuane*, ed. Beef Torrey (Jackson: University Press of Mississippi, 2007), 58.
2   Dean Kuipers, "Morality, Spirits, and Wonders," *Los Angeles Times*, December 20, 2015, F10.
3   Jim Harrison, *Off to the Side* (New York: Atlantic Monthly, 2002), 11.
4   Harrison, 18.
5   Jim Harrison, *Conversations with Jim Harrison*, ed. Robert DeMott (Jackson: University Press of Mississippi, 2019), 76.
6   Jim Harrison, *The Essential Poems* (Port Townsend, WA: Copper Canyon, 2019), 6.
7   Harrison, 7.
8   Harrison, *Off to the Side*, 19–20.
9   Harrison, 20.
10 Harrison, 23.
11 Harrison, 23.
12 Harrison, 23.
13 Harrison, 43.
14 Harrison, 43.
15 Harrison, 44.
16 Harrison, 44.
17 Harrison, 118.
18 Harrison, *Conversations*, 49.
19 Harrison, 177.
20 Harrison, 187.
21 Harrison, 235.
22 Harrison, 63.
23 Harrison, 186–187.
24 Harrison, 44.
25 Harrison, 184.
26 John Ciardi, "Everyone Writes (Bad) Poetry," *Saturday Review*, May 5, 1956, 22.
27 Jim Harrison, *Just before Dark* (New York: Houghton Mifflin, 1991), 65.
28 Harrison, *Essential Poems*, 10.
29 Harrison, 10.
30 Harrison, 10.
31 Harrison, 5.
32 Harrison, 5.

33 Harrison, *Conversations*, 138.
34 Harrison, 104.
35 Jim Harrison, "A Symposium on Secret Spaces," *Michigan Quarterly Review* 39, no. 3 (2000): 457.
36 Harrison, *Off to the Side*, 121.
37 Jim Harrison, *The Woman Lit by Fireflies* (New York: Washington Square, 1990), 184.
38 Harrison, 185.
39 Harrison, 193.
40 Harrison, 196.
41 Harrison, 235.
42 Harrison, 237.
43 Harrison, 239.
44 Harrison, 239.
45 Harrison, *Off to the Side*, 313.
46 Harrison, *Conversations*, 108.
47 Harrison, *Off to the Side*, 1.
48 Jim Harrison, "A River Never Sleeps," *Esquire*, August 1, 1976, 6.
49 Harrison, *Essential Poems*, 97.
50 Harrison, 100.
51 Harrison, 97.
52 Harrison, 102.
53 Jim Harrison, *A Good Day to Die* (New York: Delta, 1981), 19.
54 Harrison, 59.
55 Harrison, 111.
56 Harrison, 137.
57 Harrison, 138.
58 Harrison, 142.
59 Harrison, *Conversations*, 106.
60 Jim Harrison, *Legends of the Fall* (New York: Delta, 1989), 3.
61 Harrison, 3.
62 Harrison, 4.
63 Harrison, 4.
64 Harrison, 4.
65 Harrison, 13.
66 Harrison, *Conversations*, 49.
67 Harrison, 49.
68 Harrison, 49.
69 Harrison, *Just before Dark*, xii.
70 Harrison, *Conversations*, 152.

71 Jim Harrison, "Grim Reapers of the Land's Bounty," *Sports Illustrated*, October 11, 1971, 47.

72 Harrison, 43–44.

73 Harrison, *Just before Dark*, 262.

74 Harrison, *Essential Poems*, 31.

75 Harrison, *Off to the Side*, 2.

76 Harrison, *Essential Poems*, 90.

77 Harrison, 90.

78 Harrison, *Conversations*, 125.

79 Harrison, 185–186.

80 McGuane, *Conversations with Thomas McGuane*, 80.

81 Harrison, *Conversations*, 151.

82 Harrison, 129.

83 Harrison, 129.

84 Harrison, 16.

85 Harrison, 131.

86 Harrison, 19.

87 Thomas McGuane, *The Sporting Club* (New York: Vintage, 1968), 134.

88 McGuane, 134.

89 McGuane, 135.

90 Thomas McGuane, *The Longest Silence* (New York: Vintage, 1999), x.

91 McGuane, xv.

92 McGuane, xvi.

93 McGuane, 51.

94 McGuane, 75.

95 McGuane, 80.

96 McGuane, 73.

97 McGuane, 74.

98 McGuane, 73.

99 McGuane, 78.

100 McGuane, 98.

101 McGuane, 84.

102 Thomas McGuane, "Stars," *New Yorker*, June 24, 2013, https://tinyurl.com/y29gcyau.

103 McGuane.

104 McGuane.

105 McGuane.

106 McGuane, *Longest*, 252.

107 Deborah Houy, "Thomas McGuane Speaks," *Buzzworm: The Environmental Journal*, January/February 1993, 32.

108 Harrison, *Essential Poems*, 74.

109 Jim Harrison, *Selected and New Poems, 1961–1981* (New York: Dell, 1989), 90.

Chapter 5

1 Lee Bartlett, *William Everson: The Life of Brother Antoninus* (New York: New Directions, 1988), 14.

2 Bartlett, 14.

3 Robinson Jeffers, *Cawdor and Medea* (New York: New Directions, 1970), viii

4 Jeffers, vii.

5 Jeffers, x.

6 William Everson, *The Veritable Years: Poems 1949–1966* (Santa Rosa, CA: Black Sparrow, 1998), xxi.

7 William Everson [as Brother Antoninus], *Robinson Jeffers: Fragments of an Older Fury* (Berkeley, CA: Oyez, 1968), 4.

8 William Everson, *The Residual Years: Poems 1934–1948* (Santa Rosa, CA: Black Sparrow, 1997), 9.

9 Everson, 9.

10 Everson, 32.

11 Everson, 239.

12 Everson, 246.

13 Everson, 316.

14 Bartlett, *William Everson*, 92.

15 Bartlett, 104.

16 Bartlett, 34.

17 Everson, *Veritable Years*, xxii.

18 Everson, xxi.

19 Ruth Teiser, *Brother Antoninus: Poet, Printer, and Religious* (Berkeley: University of California Press, 1966), 12.

20 Harry J. Cargas, "An Interview with Brother Antoninus," *Renascence* 18, no. 3 (Spring 1966): 140.

21 Cargas, 140.

22 Cargas, 140.

23 Cargas, 140.

24 Teiser, *Brother*, 52.

25 Teiser, 51.

26 Teiser, 52.

27 Teiser, 52.

28 Everson, *Residual Years*, 361.

29 Brother Antoninus [as William Everson], "Pages from an Unpublished Autobiography," *Ramparts*, September 1962, 59.

30 Antoninus, 62.

31 Antoninus, 64.

32 Antoninus, 64.

33 Everson, *Veritable Years*, 74.

34 Everson, 35.

35 Everson, 36.

36 Everson, 52.

37 Bartlett, *William Everson*, 123.

38 Bartlett, 123.
39 Cargas, "Interview," 143–144.
40 Cargas, 144.
41 Bartlett, *William Everson*, 128–129.
42 Everson, "Pages," 44.
43 Everson, 44.
44 Everson, 56.
45 Everson, 57.
46 Everson, 57.
47 Everson, 57.
48 Father Antoninus Wall, phone interview with the author.
49 Everson, *Veritable Years*, xxxvii.
50 Everson, 20.
51 Everson, 21.
52 Everson, 22.
53 Everson, 24.
54 Everson, 33.
55 Everson, 34.
56 Everson, 17.
57 Everson, 158.
58 Everson, 158.
59 Everson, *Residual Years*, 38.

60 William Everson, "Correspondence," *Sewanee Review* 69, no. 2 (April–June 1961): 352.
61 R. Andrew Beyer, "Brother Antoninus," *Crimson*, February 21, 1963.
62 Wall, phone interview.
63 Everson, *Veritable Years*, 79.
64 Everson, 156.
65 Everson, 168.
66 Everson, 243.
67 Everson, 284.
68 William Everson, *The Integral Years: Poems 1966–1994* (Santa Rosa, CA: Black Sparrow, 2000), 8.
69 Bartlett, *William Everson*, 2.
70 William Everson, *Naked Heart* (Albuquerque: University of New Mexico Press, 1992), 106.
71 Everson, 161–162.
72 Everson, 190.
73 Wall, phone interview.
74 Everson, *Integral Years*, 236.
75 Bartlett, *William Everson*, 169.

Chapter 6

1 Merton, *Course in Desert Spirituality*, 60.
2 Merton, 60.
3 Mary Oliver, *Upstream: Selected Essays* (New York: Penguin, 2016), 10.
4 Oliver, 14.
5 Oliver, 14.
6 Oliver, 14–15.
7 Mary Oliver, "Among Wind and Time," *Sierra* 76, no. 6 (November 1991): 34.
8 Oliver, 34.
9 Oliver, 34.
10 Oliver, 34.
11 Oliver, *Upstream*, 5.
12 Oliver, 7.
13 Oliver, 7.
14 Oliver, 153.
15 Oliver, 153.
16 Oliver, "Among Wind and Time," 33.
17 Oliver, *Upstream*, 22.
18 Oliver, 61.
19 Oliver, 34.
20 Oliver, 34.
21 Oliver, 34.
22 Oliver, 111.
23 Mary Oliver, *Devotions: The Selected Poems of Mary Oliver* (New York: Penguin, 2017), 64.
24 Oliver, *Upstream*, 110.
25 Oliver, 47.

26 Oliver, 48.
27 Oliver, 48.
28 Oliver, 306.
29 Oliver, 307.
30 Oliver, 25.
31 Oliver, 25.
32 Oliver, 125.
33 Oliver, 125.
34 Oliver, 127.
35 Oliver, 136.
36 Oliver, 106.
37 Oliver, *Devotions*, 4.
38 Oliver, 4.
39 Oliver, 287.
40 Oliver, 288.
41 Oliver, 296.
42 Oliver, 298.
43 W. S. Merwin, "An Interview with W. S. Merwin," interview by Christian McEwen, *Writer's Chronicle*, February 2015.
44 W. S. Merwin, *Summer Doorways* (Washington, DC: Shoemaker & Hoard, 2005), 24.
45 Merwin, 28.
46 Merwin, 28.
47 "W. S. Merwin," *Bill Moyers Journal*, PBS, June 26, 2009, https://tinyurl.com/yybq2s66.

48 Joel Whitney, "The Garden & the Sword,"
    Tricycle, Winter 2010, https://tinyurl.com/
    y3lpl5y4.
49 Edward Hirsch, "W. S. Merwin, the Art
    of Poetry No. 38," *Paris Review*, no. 102
    (Spring 1987), https://tinyurl.com/
    y3tnmrgo.
50 Hirsch.
51 Ed Folsom and Cary Nelson, "'Fact Has
    Two Faces': An Interview with W. S.
    Merwin," *Iowa Review* 13, no. 1 (Winter
    1982): 33.
52 Folsom and Nelson, 31.
53 Folsom and Nelson, 31.
54 W. S. Merwin, "Out There," *Sunset* 201,
    no. 5 (November 1998): 42.
55 Merwin, 42.
56 Merwin, 42.
57 David L. Elliott, "An Interview with W. S.
    Merwin," *Contemporary Literature* 29, no. 1
    (Spring 1988): 3.
58 Elliott, 9.
59 Elliott, 9.
60 Folsom and Nelson, "Fact," 38–39.
61 Elliott, "Interview," 8.
62 Elliott, 9.
63 Whitney, "Garden."
64 Whitney.
65 Whitney.

66 Ed Rampell, "An Interview with W. S.
    Merwin, Poet Laureate," *Progressive*,
    October 25, 2010, https://tinyurl.com/
    y468f8mh.
67 Rampell, "Interview."
68 Whitney, "Garden."
69 Elliott, "Interview," 24.
70 Rampell, "Interview."
71 Rampell.
72 Rampell.
73 Rampell.
74 W. S. Merwin, "Letter to the Editor,"
    American Poetry Review 19, no. 2 (March/
    April 1990): 43.
75 Merwin, 43.
76 Merwin, 43.
77 Merwin, 43.
78 W. S. Merwin, "Living on an Island,"
    Sierra, September 1991, 30.
79 W. S. Merwin, *The Essential W. S. Merwin*,
    ed. Michael Wiegers (Port Townsend, WA:
    Copper Canyon, 2017), 51.
80 Merwin, 163.
81 Merwin, 107.
82 Merwin, 302.
83 Merwin, 57.
84 Merwin, 207.
85 Merwin, 207.
86 Merwin, 304.

Conclusion

1   Rüdiger Safranski, *Martin Heidegger:
    Between Good and Evil* (Cambridge, MA:
    Harvard University Press, 1999), 143.
2   Adam Sharr, *Heidegger's Hut* (Cambridge,
    MA: MIT Press, 2006), 44.
3   Martin Heidegger, *Philosophical and
    Political Writings*, ed. Manfred Stassen
    (New York: Continuum, 2003), 16.
4   Heidegger, 16.
5   Heidegger, 16.
6   Heidegger, 16.
7   Heidegger, 17.
8   Martin Heidegger, *Poetry, Language,
    Thought*, trans. Albert Hofstadter (New
    York: HarperPerennial, 2001), 51.
9   Martin Heidegger, *On Time and Being*,
    trans. Joan Stambaugh (Chicago:
    University of Chicago Press, 2002), 65.
10 Heidegger, *Poetry*, 51.
11 Safranski, *Martin*, 7.
12 Toni Morrison, *Beloved* (New York: Plume,
    1988), 15.

13 Morrison, 17.
14 Morrison, 39.
15 Morrison, 50.
16 Morrison, 85.
17 Morrison, 84.
18 Morrison, 86.
19 Heidegger, *Poetry*, 51.
20 Heidegger, *On Time and Being*, 65.
21 Morrison, *Beloved*, 87.
22 Morrison, 87.
23 Morrison, 87.
24 Morrison, 88.
25 Morrison, 89.
26 Morrison, 89.
27 Morrison, 89.
28 Morrison, 95.
29 Morrison, 261.
30 Morrison, 261.
31 Morrison, 275.
32 John McPhee, *The John McPhee Reader*, ed.
    William L. Howarth (New York: Vintage,
    1978), 80.

33 McPhee, 81.

34 Rick Bass, *Why I Came West* (New York: Houghton Mifflin, 2008), 33.

35 Bass, 33.

36 Edward Abbey, *Desert Solitaire* (New York: Simon & Schuster, 1990), 166.

37 Abbey, 166–167.

38 Abbey, 184.

39 Abbey, 194.

40 Abbey, 243.

41 John Fowles, *The Tree* (New York: Ecco, 2010), x.

42 Fowles, xi.

43 Fowles, 3.

44 Fowles, 7.

45 Fowles, 25.

46 Fowles, 27.

47 Fowles, 29.

48 Fowles, 39.

49 Fowles, 51.

50 Fowles, 87.

51 Robert Macfarlane, *The Wild Places* (New York: Penguin, 2007), 157.

52 Macfarlane, 157.

53 Macfarlane, 157.

54 Fowles, *Tree*, 91.

55 Pope Francis, *Encyclical Letter Laudato si' of the Holy Father Francis on Care for Our Common Home* (Vatican City: Vatican Press, 2015), 3, https://tinyurl.com/yae5534n.

56 Pope Francis, 11.

57 Pope Francis, 158–159.

58 Pope Francis, 159.

59 Pope Francis, 159.

60 Hopkins, *Poems*, 51.

Index

Abbey, Edward, 75, 125–26
    Desert Solitaire, 126
Abbey of Gethsemani, 17, 48
Abraham, 16, 26
Adam, 13
Alighieri, Dante, xiii
    Inferno, The, xiii, 67
Altdorfer, Albrecht, 9
    Two Saints John, The, 9
American Poetry Review, 113
Ammonas, Abba, 15
Andrew, Abba, 20
Arizona, 64
Arsenius, Abba, 18
Athanasius, 21–22
    Life of Antony, 21–22
Augustine, 8, 89

Balzac, Honoré de, 126
Bannus, 6,
Bartlett, Lee, 86
Bass, Rick, 125–26
Baudelaire, Charles, 22
Bernheimer, Richard, 10
Berry, Thomas, xvi–xvii, xviii
Berry, Wendell, 47–55, 56, 61–62,
    73
Blaise, 8–9
Bly, Robert, 110
Boff, Leonardo, 128–29
Bonaparte, Joseph, 124
Bosch, Hieronymus, 59
    Garden of Earthly Delights, The, 59
Breughel, Pieter, 22
Bridges, Robert, 36, 39, 42–44

Brooks, Paul, xi
Burton, Naomi, 95

Caesarea, Basil of, 20
California, 83–99
Catholic Worker, 48, 91–92
Ciardi, John, 67
Connolly, Cyril, 86
Cooper, Susan Fenimore, xviii
    Rural Hours, xviii
Cronon, William, xv
Cyril of Jerusalem, 7

Daniel, 10
David, 3
Day, Dorothy, 48, 91
Deloria, Jr., Vine, xvi
Desert Fathers and Mothers, 15–26, 101,
    126
Deuteronomy, 2
Dickey, James, 94–95
Diolcos, Abba John of, 20
Dixon, Richard Watson, 40
Duncan, Robert, 88

Elijah, 3, 5, 7, 12
Elizabeth, 4
Emerson, Ralph Waldo, xvi
Eucherius of Lyons, 20
Everson, William (Brother Antoninus),
    83–99, 106, 110
    Crooked Lines of God, The, 93–94
    Hazards of Holiness, The, 96
    Integral Years, The, 97
    Masculine Dead, The, 86
    Residual Years, The, 87, 94, 97
    River-Root, 96
    Rose of Solitude, The, 97

San Joaquin, 86
These Are the Ravens, 86
Triptych for the Living, 91
Veritable Years, The, 97
Exodus, 1
Ezekiel, xii

Fabilli, Mary, 88–90
Flaubert, Gustave, 22–25
    Madame Bovary, 22
    Temptation of Saint Anthony, The,
      22–25
Florida, 72, 79
Foucault, Michael, 22–23
Fourteen Holy Helpers, 9
Fowles, John, 127–28
    Tree, The, 127–28
Franklin, Benjamin, 124

Gabriel (angel), 4
garden of Eden, 1, 3, 19
Gardner, John, 72
Gatta, John, xv
Gelpi, Albert, 87
Genesis, 19
Gethsemane, 26
Gioia, Dana, 84
Great Salt Lake, 48, 57

Harrison, Jim, 63–77, 81
    A Good Day to Die, 72–74
    Just Before Dark, 74
    Off to the Side, 71
    Plain Song, 68
    Returning to Earth, 76
Harrowing of Hell, 7
Hawai'i, 111–14
Hearn, Lafcadio, 22

Heidegger, Martin, 117–19, 121
  Being and Time, 117
Hermits of Saint William, 11
Herod, 6–7, 10, 93
Herodias, 6
Hopkins, Gerard Manley, 27–45, 48, 93,
  96, 105, 106, 115, 129
Hotchkiss, Bill, 98

Idaho, 73
Isaiah, xii, 3, 12, 66, 95

Jacob, xii
Jeffers, Robinson, 84–85, 92, 94
  Cawdor and Medea, 85
Jeremiah, 95
Jericho, 5
Jerome, 8
Jersey Devil, The, 123–24
Jesus, x, 1, 5–7, 12–13, 17–18, 21, 26,
  27, 28, 34, 38, 40, 44, 45, 49, 57,
  67, 77, 89, 93–94, 106, 109, 112,
  129
Job, 96
Johnson's Wonder-Working Providence, 49
John the Baptist, 1, 4–13, 17
Josephus, Flavius, 6, 10
  Jewish Antiquities, 6
Judea, 1, 5–6

Kelhoffer, James A., 4
Kentucky, 47–56
Kierkegaard, Soren, 67

Lanes Landing Farm, 48
Laudato si', 128–29
Laughlin, James, 89
Lawrence, D. H., 60

Leeds, Daniel, 123
Levertov, Denise, 48, 68
Lévi-Strauss, Claude, xvii
Lopez, Barry, 126
Luke (Gospel), 112

Macfarlane, Robert, 128
Maleval, William of, 11
Mark (Gospel), 4–5, 7, 12
Mary, 4, 37–38
Massachusetts, 77, 104
Massachusetts Review, The, 102
Mattathias, 3
Matthew (Gospel), xiii, 5
Maurin, Peter, 91
McClure, Michael, 96
McCool, Carroll, 91
McGuane, Thomas, 63–64, 76–81
  Sporting Club, The, 77–78
McPhee, John, 123
Meatyard, Ralph Eugene, 50
Merton, Thomas, xvi, 17–21, 25, 47–50,
  95, 101
Merwin, William Stage, 102, 108–15
Merwin Palm Forest, 113
Michigan, 64–68, 77–79
Mitty, John, 95
Monks Pond, 48
Montana, 64, 79
Morrison, Toni, 119–22
  Beloved, 119–22
Muir, John, xii, xv–xvi
  Our National Parks, xii

Nash, Roderick, xi, xiii,
Nebuchadnezzar, 10, 24
Netras, Abba, 20
New Jersey, ix–x, xviii–xix, 108, 122–25

Newman, John Henry, 28
New York, xviii, 48, 58, 108
Nouwen, Henri, 15, 18, 20
Numbers, 1–2

Oelschlaeger, Max, xi
Ohio, 103–4, 119–20
Oliver, Mary, 102–8, 115
    Devotions, 107
Oregon, 87
Origen, 7

Paul (apostle), xiii, 68
Pope Francis, 128–29
Porter, Joy, xvi
Poulson, Edwa, 85, 87, 90
Protevangelium of James, The, 4
Psalms, 2

Rexroth, Kenneth, 86, 88–89
Rickson, Susanna, 97
Rodriguez, Richard, 16, 26

Saint Anthony the Great, 15, 21–25, 28
Saint Francis of Assisi, 128–29
Saint John Climacus, 25–26
    Holy Ladder, The, 25–26
Saint Martin of Tours, 8
Sartre, Jean-Paul, 67
Saturday Review, 67

Saul, 3
Second Maccabees, 16
Severus, Sulpicius, 7–8
Sewanee Review, 94
Snyder, Gary, xvii
Stegner, Wallace, x–xi

Tannlund, Rose, 97
Thoreau, Henry David, xvii–xviii, 50,
    109

Utah, x, 47–48, 55–60, 125–26

Verba seniorum, 18

Wall, Father Antoninus, 92, 95, 97–98
Wao Kele O Puna, 113
Whitman, Walt, 103, 109
Wilderness Act, x
Williams, George H., 1–2
Williams, Raymond, xiv,
Williams, Terry Tempest, 47, 55–62, 73,
    110
    Refuge: An Unnatural History of
        Family and Place, 48, 57–58
Wordsworth, William, xiii–xv
    Lyrical Ballads, xiii–xiv
Wyoming, 72

Zechariah, 4